Resonate, Don't Just Connect:
Fostering Creative, Community-Driven Relationships in Louisville and Kentucky

Resonate, Don't Just Connect:
Fostering Creative, Community-Driven Relationships in Louisville and Kentucky

Contents

Copyright © 2024 by Di Tran Enterprise 4

Introduction: Resonate with Purpose: Building Lasting, Community-Driven Connections in Louisville and Beyond 6

Chapter 1: The Power of Genuine Networking – Building Meaningful Relationships, Not Just Contacts 15

Chapter 2: First Impressions That Last – How to Leave a Lasting Impact When Meeting People for the First Time . 24

Chapter 3: Navigating Business Events and Conferences – Tips on Maximizing Value from Industry Gatherings 36

Chapter 4: The Follow-Up Formula – How to Maintain and Nurture Relationships Long After the First Meeting .. 48

Chapter 5: Networking in the Digital Age – Utilizing Platforms Like LinkedIn and Social Media to Expand Your Circle 62

Chapter 6: Leveraging Your Network for Business Growth – Turning Connections into Opportunities 79

Chapter 7: Creating a Win-Win Culture – Building Long-Term Partnerships that Benefit All Parties 95

Chapter 8: Overcoming Networking Anxiety – How to Approach Networking When You're an Introvert or Uncomfortable 112

Chapter 9: The Business of Giving – The Importance of Offering Value Before Asking for Favors 128

Resonate, Don't Just Connect:
Fostering Creative, Community-Driven Relationships in Louisville and Kentucky

Chapter 10: Measuring the ROI of Networking – Tracking the Real Business Outcomes of Your Connections 162

The End..180

Resonate, Don't Just Connect:
Fostering Creative, Community-Driven Relationships in Louisville and Kentucky

Copyright © 2024 by Di Tran Enterprise

All rights reserved. No part of this publication may be reproduced, distributed, or transmitted in any form or by any means, including photocopying, recording, or other electronic or mechanical methods, without the prior written permission of the publisher, except in the case of brief quotations embodied in critical reviews and certain other noncommercial uses permitted by copyright law.

The information contained in this book is intended for educational and inspirational purposes only. It is sold with the understanding that the publisher and author are not engaged in rendering psychological, counseling, or other professional services. If expert assistance is required, the services of a competent professional should be sought.

This publication is designed to provide accurate and authoritative information in regard to the subject matter covered. It is presented with the understanding that the author and publisher are not engaged in rendering personal, professional, or any other kind of advice. The reader should consult his or her medical, legal, financial, or other competent professional before adopting any of the suggestions in this book or drawing inferences from it.

Resonate, Don't Just Connect:
Fostering Creative, Community-Driven Relationships in Louisville and Kentucky

This publication reflects the author's views, experiences, and opinions. It is intended to provide helpful and informative material on the subjects addressed in the publication. The author and publisher shall have neither liability nor responsibility to any person or entity with respect to any loss, damage, or injury caused, or alleged to be caused, directly or indirectly by the information contained in this book.

While the author has made every effort to ensure the accuracy and completeness of the information contained in this publication, we assume no responsibility for errors, inaccuracies, omissions, or any inconsistency herein. Any slights of people or organizations are unintentional.

Resonate, Don't Just Connect:
Fostering Creative, Community-Driven Relationships in Louisville and Kentucky

Introduction: Resonate with Purpose: Building Lasting, Community-Driven Connections in Louisville and Beyond

I am Di Tran, a person who was once shy beyond comprehension, someone who grew up with a profound fear of engaging with people. As a child, I could barely open my mouth to speak, and I vividly remember a time when I was 10 years old, attending a Catholic boarding school run by nuns. One day, I was assigned to read a passage from the Bible in church—a daunting task for a boy who had never dared to speak aloud in class. I was the quintessential introvert, terrified of being seen or heard. Yet, even in my silence, I learned to observe the world around me. I paid close attention to people's behavior, their interactions, and their unspoken words. While I stayed quiet on the outside, inside I was absorbing life's lessons, understanding how people moved through the world, how they connected, and how they communicated.

Now, at the age of 42, after decades of personal and professional growth, I stand in a vastly different place. I still reflect on my introverted tendencies, but today, I realize they were never a weakness. Instead, they allowed

Resonate, Don't Just Connect:
Fostering Creative, Community-Driven Relationships in Louisville and Kentucky

me to develop a deep capacity for empathy, observation, and reflection—qualities that have shaped my relationships, my business, and my spiritual journey. My life is a testament to the power of human connection, and I have learned that true engagement with others comes not from speaking the most, but from listening the best. When I do speak, people often tell me that my words are those of a man much older than my years. I am 42, but I have been told that I think and speak like someone ten or twenty years older, someone who has lived and loved deeply, someone who has reflected on the complexities of life.

Today, I often find myself gravitating toward people in their 60s and beyond. These are the people who have lived through the trials of life, who have learned the delicate art of resonating with others. They are humble, patient, and wise. They have mastered the ability to engage with people on a deeper level, to add value rather than extract it, to give more than they receive. I find myself addicted to this kind of crowd because, through them, I learn not just about business or success, but about life, love, and God.

One of the most significant influences in my life has been the Rotary Club of Louisville. As one of the few Asians and one of the youngest regular attendees, I stand out. Yet, what I have gained from attending these meetings transcends any superficial differences. The people I have

Resonate, Don't Just Connect:
Fostering Creative, Community-Driven Relationships in Louisville and Kentucky

met through Rotary and other political and business associations have taught me that success is not just about networking or making connections—it's about resonating with others on a human level. It's about understanding their stories, their struggles, their dreams. It's about speaking not to be heard, but to be understood. My first American mentor, Thomas Ransdell, instilled this lesson in me early on. He would often say, "Speak to be understood, not to speak for the sake of speaking." His words have stayed with me throughout my journey, guiding me in every interaction.

Later, another mentor, Thomas Noland, who served as Chief Communication Officer at Humana, deepened my understanding of this principle. He taught me that the key to effective communication—whether in writing, verbally, or through body language—lies in the ability to resonate with others on a human level. It's about making people feel seen, heard, and valued. Noland taught me that when you communicate from a place of empathy and understanding, people align with you more naturally. They trust you. They feel connected to you. And in that space of mutual respect and resonance, creativity and collaboration flourish.

I was also fortunate to learn from Brian Keinsley, Senior Vice President of Humana's IT department, who guided me through the complex political landscape of corporate life. Brian wasn't just a mentor in business; he was

Resonate, Don't Just Connect:
Fostering Creative, Community-Driven Relationships in Louisville and Kentucky

someone who understood the deeper importance of relationships. He, too, emphasized the importance of resonating with others, of creating value in every interaction. Together, these three mentors—Thomas Ransdell, Thomas Noland, and Brian Keinsley—shaped not just my career, but my entire approach to life. They have since passed on, leaving this earth to return to God. But their wisdom remains with me, guiding me in all I do.

As I write this, I also reflect on my new friend, Rick Dye, who has become a mentor and partner in our mission to solve affordable housing. Rick, a former CEO of a bank and a man who humbly calls himself "a banker," often advises me on my way of communicating. We are working together to build independent, essential homes—480-square-foot houses—to address the affordable housing crisis. Rick shared with me one of the most humbling insights I've ever received: "People tend to like to speak with those who look like them. You are too different. You are beyond the language that you use to speak; you are heavy in your accent, and your word usage could be a lot better."

For the first time, I had a mentor tell me this truth so directly. And yet, I accepted this feedback wholeheartedly because I knew that it came from a place of care and a desire to see me grow. I also accept that God has given me talents and capabilities beyond the limitations of language or accent. I often ask myself: even if I spoke in

Resonate, Don't Just Connect:
Fostering Creative, Community-Driven Relationships in Louisville and Kentucky

Vietnamese today, would I be able to resonate with people? The answer, more often than not, is no. It is not just about the language or the words I use. Yes, those things matter, but the core of communication and networking lies in the ability to resonate with others. It's about making a connection that transcends words, touching the soul. And this is true for all aspects of business.

No one speaks with me today simply because I speak English well or because I am exceptional in any particular skill. In fact, I do not consider myself to be great at anything. But there is one thing I know for sure and strive to improve daily: I have a mentality centered on adding value. I exist to add value, and my connection to anyone is driven by the same purpose. I connect with others to add value to their lives first, and if they happen to add value to mine in return, then that is the beauty of God's work. This is the essence of life that we often forget: we are here to serve others, just as Jesus washed the feet of His disciples.

As I look back on my life and the relationships I have built, I see a clear pattern—one that is rooted in the philosophy of giving, loving, and resonating with others. This book is an exploration of that philosophy. It's about how we can build creative, community-driven relationships that go beyond mere networking. It's about

Resonate, Don't Just Connect:

Fostering Creative, Community-Driven Relationships in Louisville and Kentucky

how we can learn to resonate with others, not just on a surface level, but in a way that touches the soul.

In all of my books, I have written about the importance of service, of adding value to the lives of others, and of approaching every interaction with a spirit of love and generosity. Whether it's in business, personal relationships, or community engagement, the principle remains the same: we are here to serve one another. We are here to add value, to lift each other up, and to create spaces where creativity, collaboration, and love can flourish.

In the pages that follow, I will share what I have learned about the art of human connection. I will draw from my experiences growing up as a shy, introverted child in Vietnam, navigating the complexities of life in America, and finding my voice in the business world. I will share stories from my time with the Rotary Club of Louisville, my experiences with mentors who have shaped my life, and my reflections on the power of humanization in communication.

This book is not just about building networks—it's about building relationships that matter. It's about learning to resonate with others on a level that goes beyond transactions or business deals. It's about fostering connections that are rooted in empathy, understanding, and mutual respect. In today's world, where so much of

Resonate, Don't Just Connect:
Fostering Creative, Community-Driven Relationships in Louisville and Kentucky

our interaction is superficial and self-serving, I believe there is a deep need for a return to authentic, value-driven relationships. This is the essence of what I have learned, and it is what I hope to share with you in this book.

As you read through the chapters, I encourage you to reflect on your own relationships—both personal and professional. How do you connect with others? How do you add value to their lives? Are you resonating with people in a way that fosters true connection, or are you merely exchanging pleasantries and favors? My hope is that this book will inspire you to deepen your relationships, to approach every interaction with a spirit of love and service, and to build a network that not only supports your success but also contributes to the greater good of your community.

In closing, I am reminded of a simple but profound truth: we are all interconnected. Our lives are woven together in ways we may never fully understand. When we take the time to truly connect with one another—to listen, to share, to serve—we create something beautiful. We create a world where creativity, collaboration, and love thrive. And that, I believe, is the true purpose of life.

This is my story, my journey, and my belief in the power of human connection. I invite you to join me in this exploration of what it means to truly resonate with others

Resonate, Don't Just Connect:
Fostering Creative, Community-Driven Relationships in Louisville and Kentucky

and to build relationships that bring lasting value to the world.

Resonate, Don't Just Connect:
Fostering Creative, Community-Driven Relationships in Louisville and Kentucky

Chapter 1: The Power of Genuine Networking – Building Meaningful Relationships, Not Just Contacts

In the world of business, especially in a city like Louisville, Kentucky, the concept of networking is often reduced to handing out business cards, sending LinkedIn requests, or attending a few networking events. While these actions might help increase your contact list, they don't necessarily help you build the kind of meaningful, lasting relationships that can truly transform your career and your life. The real power of networking lies in forging genuine connections—connections that go beyond the superficial exchange of information and instead foster trust, collaboration, and mutual growth.

Louisville, despite its smaller size compared to larger metropolitan cities like New York or Los Angeles, is unique. It is home to a significant number of Fortune 500 companies and major industries like healthcare, logistics, and manufacturing. With companies like Yum! Brands, Humana, and Papa John's headquartered here, Louisville is a city where networking plays a vital role in building a successful career. In a community like this, where word-of-mouth and reputation are still powerful forces, it's not

Resonate, Don't Just Connect:
Fostering Creative, Community-Driven Relationships in Louisville and Kentucky

enough to simply know people. You need to build meaningful relationships that stand the test of time. Networking in Louisville is about being genuine, creating connections based on trust, and working to add value to the people you meet.

This chapter will explore how to build such meaningful relationships, focusing on the difference between simply collecting contacts and cultivating lasting, impactful professional connections. You'll learn how the power of genuine networking can lead to incredible opportunities, both in business and in life, and how a city like Louisville provides the perfect landscape for fostering these connections.

Understanding the Louisville Landscape

Louisville is a small city with big-city ambitions. Its economy is diverse, and its key industries—healthcare, bourbon, logistics, and manufacturing—are the backbone of the region. It's a city that takes pride in its community spirit and sense of connectedness. In fact, many business leaders in Louisville will tell you that the relationships you build here are often the deciding factor in whether you succeed.

Because of Louisville's unique combination of being a tight-knit community while also being a city of global importance due to its Fortune 500 companies, building meaningful relationships is more crucial here than in other

Resonate, Don't Just Connect:
Fostering Creative, Community-Driven Relationships in Louisville and Kentucky

places. People talk, and reputations are built over time, based on the quality of interactions you have. If you're seen as someone who is only out to advance your own agenda or take without giving back, word can spread quickly. But, if you're seen as someone who cares about others, contributes to the community, and adds value, those same conversations will work in your favor, often opening doors you didn't even know existed.

In Louisville, the power of genuine networking lies in being authentic, adding value, and investing in long-term relationships. It's about playing the long game, where the focus is on building a reputation as someone who genuinely cares about others' success, as well as your own.

Building Authentic Connections

At the heart of genuine networking is authenticity. When people talk about the difference between someone who is a true networker and someone who is simply building contacts, the distinction usually comes down to this one word. Authenticity means being honest about who you are, what you bring to the table, and what you're looking for in relationships.

In a city like Louisville, where relationships can open up long-term opportunities, being authentic allows people to trust you. Trust is the foundation of any meaningful connection, especially in business. If you're only looking

Resonate, Don't Just Connect:
Fostering Creative, Community-Driven Relationships in Louisville and Kentucky

to collect business cards and call people when you need something, it's unlikely that you'll build the kind of relationships that matter. On the other hand, when you're authentic, people are more likely to want to help you, work with you, and introduce you to others in their network.

To build authentic connections, you must first understand your own goals and values. What drives you? What are your strengths, and how can you add value to the people you meet? When you're clear on these things, it becomes easier to approach new relationships from a place of sincerity, rather than simply trying to "sell" yourself or extract something from others. And this is particularly important in a city like Louisville, where people tend to work closely with each other over long periods of time. Your reputation and your authenticity are assets that will carry you far.

Giving Before You Take

One of the most important principles of genuine networking is to always offer value before you ask for anything in return. Too many people approach networking with a mindset of "What can this person do for me?" rather than "How can I help this person?"

In a community-focused city like Louisville, giving before you take is essential. Whether you're new to the city or have been working here for years, the key to

Resonate, Don't Just Connect:
Fostering Creative, Community-Driven Relationships in Louisville and Kentucky

building strong relationships is to find ways to contribute. This might mean offering to help someone with a project, introducing them to a valuable contact, or sharing resources that could benefit their business. When you give first, you establish yourself as someone who is genuinely interested in helping others succeed, which builds trust and strengthens relationships.

This approach is particularly important in Louisville, where industries are interconnected, and word travels fast. If you're known as someone who helps others without expecting anything in return, people will be more likely to recommend you, introduce you to their contacts, and seek you out for opportunities.

Consider the story of how many local entrepreneurs in Louisville have built their networks by first offering their expertise for free or low cost. By providing value to others, they established their reputations as generous and knowledgeable professionals, and as a result, their businesses grew through referrals and long-term partnerships.

The Importance of Consistency

Building meaningful relationships takes time, and consistency is key. This is another area where many people falter in their networking efforts. They attend one event, make a few connections, and then never follow up. Genuine networking requires ongoing effort—you have to

Resonate, Don't Just Connect:
Fostering Creative, Community-Driven Relationships in Louisville and Kentucky

keep showing up and nurturing the relationships you've built.

In Louisville, it's important to stay connected to your network through consistent communication and follow-up. This doesn't mean constantly asking for favors or trying to sell your services. Instead, it means checking in with people, asking how you can support them, and keeping them updated on your own progress. Whether it's a quick email, a phone call, or a coffee meeting, the key is to stay top-of-mind without being intrusive.

This consistency builds trust over time and shows people that you're committed to the relationship, not just looking for short-term gains. In Louisville, where industries are interconnected and relationships are often long-term, consistency is essential for maintaining and growing your network.

Building Win-Win Relationships

One of the hallmarks of genuine networking is the ability to create win-win relationships. This means finding ways to benefit both parties in a relationship, rather than just focusing on your own gain. In a city like Louisville, where collaboration is key to success, building win-win relationships can lead to incredible opportunities.

To build win-win relationships, start by understanding what the other person values and what their goals are.

Resonate, Don't Just Connect:
Fostering Creative, Community-Driven Relationships in Louisville and Kentucky

How can you help them achieve those goals? At the same time, be clear about your own objectives, and look for ways to align your interests. When both parties benefit from the relationship, it becomes stronger and more sustainable over time.

In Louisville's business community, win-win relationships often lead to partnerships, collaborations, and long-term success. Whether you're working with someone in your industry or across different sectors, the ability to create mutual value is one of the most powerful tools you have in networking.

A real-life example of this in Louisville can be seen in the collaboration between local tech companies and logistics firms. By working together and leveraging each other's strengths, these companies have been able to solve complex problems, grow their businesses, and make Louisville a hub for innovation in logistics. This kind of collaboration wouldn't be possible without the trust and mutual benefit that comes from genuine, win-win relationships.

The Long-Term Benefits of Meaningful Relationships

When you focus on building meaningful relationships rather than just collecting contacts, the long-term benefits can be substantial. In a city like Louisville, where connections can open doors to new opportunities, having

Resonate, Don't Just Connect:
Fostering Creative, Community-Driven Relationships in Louisville and Kentucky

a strong network of genuine relationships can lead to new business ventures, partnerships, job offers, and more.

Meaningful relationships are also more resilient than superficial ones. In business, you'll inevitably face challenges and setbacks. When you have genuine relationships with people who trust you, they'll be more likely to support you during tough times. Whether it's offering advice, providing resources, or simply being there to listen, your network can be an invaluable source of support when you need it most.

Additionally, meaningful relationships often lead to opportunities that you wouldn't have been able to access on your own. When people trust you and see the value you bring, they'll be more likely to introduce you to their own networks, recommend you for projects, and offer opportunities that can take your career to the next level.

Conclusion: The Power of Genuine Networking in Louisville

Louisville may be a small city in terms of population, but its business community is vibrant, diverse, and full of opportunities. The key to unlocking these opportunities lies in building meaningful, genuine relationships. By focusing on authenticity, giving before you take, being consistent, and creating win-win relationships, you can build a network that not only supports your career but also enhances your life.

Resonate, Don't Just Connect:
Fostering Creative, Community-Driven Relationships in Louisville and Kentucky

Networking in Louisville is about more than just business cards and LinkedIn connections—it's about building a community of people who trust and support each other. In this tight-knit, interconnected city, the relationships you build can have a lasting impact on your career and your life. By investing in genuine, long-term connections, you can become a valuable member of the Louisville business community, unlocking new opportunities and creating a strong foundation for success.

Resonate, Don't Just Connect:
Fostering Creative, Community-Driven Relationships in Louisville and Kentucky

Chapter 2: First Impressions That Last – How to Leave a Lasting Impact When Meeting People for the First Time

First impressions have the power to shape your entire relationship with someone. Whether it's a business meeting, a networking event, or a casual encounter, the way you present yourself during those first few minutes often determines the nature of the connection that follows. In Kentucky, a state known for its warmth, hospitality, and strong sense of community, first impressions are critical. Kentuckians value authenticity, sincerity, and respect. Being able to leave a lasting positive impact when meeting someone for the first time is not just about what you say, but how you make people feel.

Kentucky may be famous for its bluegrass, bourbon, and thoroughbred horses, but it's also known for the relationships that are built on trust and camaraderie. These values permeate the business world, making it vital to master the art of leaving a great first impression. Whether you're meeting people in cities like Louisville or Lexington or connecting with folks in more rural parts of the state, understanding how to make a memorable first impression is a crucial skill. This chapter will guide you

Resonate, Don't Just Connect:
Fostering Creative, Community-Driven Relationships in Louisville and Kentucky

through strategies for making a lasting impact that goes beyond surface-level interactions and builds meaningful relationships from the start.

The Importance of First Impressions in Kentucky's Business Culture

Kentucky's economy is built on industries that thrive on strong relationships—bourbon, horse racing, manufacturing, healthcare, and agriculture, to name a few. In these sectors, trust is paramount, and often the foundation of that trust begins with the first impression you make. Whether you're sitting down with potential investors, meeting a local farmer to discuss a business deal, or shaking hands with fellow entrepreneurs at a conference, the way you present yourself from the very start can either open doors or shut them.

Unlike larger, more anonymous urban centers where you may meet someone once and never see them again, in Kentucky, the business community is closely knit. People talk, and word about your character and professionalism spreads quickly. This makes first impressions even more important here than in other parts of the country. Establishing credibility and showing respect from the outset are key components of leaving a lasting impact.

Preparing for Your First Meeting

Resonate, Don't Just Connect:
Fostering Creative, Community-Driven Relationships in Louisville and Kentucky

Before you walk into any meeting or networking event, preparation is key. This means not only understanding who you are meeting but also reflecting on how you want to present yourself. In Kentucky, where traditions and values often play a significant role in business, it's essential to be mindful of how you approach people. The following strategies can help you prepare to make a great first impression:

1. **Know Your Audience**: Do your homework on the people you're meeting. In a state like Kentucky, people appreciate when you take the time to understand their background, their business, and their values. This doesn't mean you have to know everything, but being familiar with key details about their industry or their work shows respect and interest. If you're meeting someone from the bourbon industry, for example, it helps to have a basic understanding of the process or the significance of bourbon in Kentucky's economy.

2. **Be Punctual**: Being on time is a sign of respect, and it's especially important in Kentucky's business culture, where personal relationships are highly valued. Arriving late can be seen as disrespectful or disorganized, and it can set a negative tone for the rest of your interaction. Always aim to arrive early or on time, showing

Resonate, Don't Just Connect:
Fostering Creative, Community-Driven Relationships in Louisville and Kentucky

that you respect the other person's time and are serious about the meeting.

3. **Dress the Part**: While Kentucky business attire may vary depending on the region and the industry, it's important to dress appropriately for the occasion. In larger cities like Louisville or Lexington, more formal business attire is common in corporate settings. However, in more rural areas or industries like agriculture, people might appreciate a more casual and practical approach to attire. Regardless of the setting, dressing neatly and professionally helps convey that you take the meeting seriously.

4. **Mindset Matters**: Before walking into any meeting or event, take a few moments to clear your mind and set a positive, confident tone. In Kentucky, people value humility but also appreciate confidence. Being present, relaxed, and engaged is crucial for making a strong first impression.

The Power of Body Language

Research has shown that non-verbal cues like body language play a huge role in how we are perceived, especially during first meetings. In Kentucky, where personal connections and face-to-face interactions are still

Resonate, Don't Just Connect:
Fostering Creative, Community-Driven Relationships in Louisville and Kentucky

valued, the way you carry yourself can communicate confidence, respect, and sincerity.

1. **Eye Contact**: In Kentucky, as in many other places, eye contact is a sign of respect and trustworthiness. When you meet someone for the first time, make sure to maintain eye contact throughout the conversation. Avoid looking away or down at your phone, as this can make you seem disengaged or disinterested.

2. **Firm Handshake**: The handshake remains a timeless gesture of greeting, particularly in Kentucky's business culture. A firm, confident handshake conveys confidence and sincerity. Be sure not to overdo it with an overly strong grip, but also avoid a weak handshake, which can suggest a lack of confidence or enthusiasm.

3. **Posture and Presence**: Stand tall and maintain good posture. Slouching or fidgeting can convey disinterest or nervousness, while standing confidently with your shoulders back signals that you are engaged and attentive. In Kentucky, where people often prefer direct and honest communication, your posture can speak volumes about your level of interest and professionalism.

4. **Smile**: A genuine smile can go a long way in making a positive first impression. Kentuckians,

known for their Southern hospitality, appreciate warmth and friendliness. A sincere smile shows that you are approachable, open, and ready to engage.

Listening Is Just as Important as Speaking

One of the most effective ways to leave a lasting first impression is by being a good listener. In Kentucky, where conversations often extend beyond business into more personal territory, people appreciate when you take the time to really listen and engage with what they're saying.

1. **Active Listening**: Active listening involves more than just hearing what the other person is saying—it's about engaging with their words and showing that you understand and value their perspective. Nodding occasionally, asking follow-up questions, and offering thoughtful responses are all signs that you are actively engaged in the conversation.

2. **Don't Interrupt**: While it might seem obvious, interrupting someone while they are speaking is one of the quickest ways to make a poor impression. In Kentucky's business culture, where respect and patience are valued, allowing the other person to finish their thought before responding is essential.

Resonate, Don't Just Connect:
Fostering Creative, Community-Driven Relationships in Louisville and Kentucky

3. **Ask Meaningful Questions**: Show that you are not just passively listening but are genuinely interested in the conversation. Asking open-ended, thoughtful questions demonstrates curiosity and a desire to understand the other person better. This can help deepen the conversation and show that you are interested in building a meaningful connection.

Be Genuine and Sincere

In a place like Kentucky, where relationships are often built on trust, sincerity is key. People here can often spot insincerity a mile away, so trying to fake interest or enthusiasm won't get you far. The best way to make a positive first impression is to be yourself and to be genuine in your interactions.

1. **Don't Pretend to Know Everything**: It's perfectly fine to admit when you don't know something. In fact, in Kentucky's culture of humility and authenticity, being upfront about your knowledge gaps can actually help you build trust. People appreciate honesty and are more likely to help you if you are sincere about what you know and don't know.

2. **Share Your Story**: One of the most effective ways to build rapport quickly is by sharing a bit of your personal story. In Kentucky, where family

and personal history often play a big role in people's lives, sharing where you come from and what you care about can help establish a deeper connection. Whether you're from Kentucky or not, people will appreciate learning more about who you are as a person, not just a professional.

3. **Follow Through on Promises**: If you tell someone you'll follow up with them after the meeting or send them a resource, make sure you do it. Following through on your promises is one of the quickest ways to build trust and leave a lasting impression. In Kentucky's tight-knit business community, your reputation will often precede you, so being known as someone who keeps their word is invaluable.

Handling Introductions with Confidence

Introductions are often the very first step in making a great first impression. Whether you're introducing yourself at a networking event or being introduced to someone else, the way you handle that moment can set the tone for the entire interaction.

1. **Introduce Yourself Clearly**: When introducing yourself, make sure to speak clearly and confidently. In Kentucky's business culture, clarity and professionalism are valued, so take a moment to clearly state your name, your role, and

Resonate, Don't Just Connect:
Fostering Creative, Community-Driven Relationships in Louisville and Kentucky

any relevant information about your work. Avoid rambling or overloading the person with too much information right away—keep it simple and direct.

2. **Pay Attention to Names**: In Kentucky, where personal connections are key, remembering people's names can go a long way in making a positive impression. When you meet someone for the first time, make a conscious effort to remember their name and use it throughout the conversation. If you're worried about forgetting, try repeating their name shortly after they introduce themselves, such as, "It's great to meet you, John."

3. **Be Respectful in Group Settings**: If you're being introduced to a group, take a moment to greet each person individually, rather than just addressing the group as a whole. This shows that you value each person in the room and helps create a more personal connection. In Kentucky, where hospitality is important, acknowledging everyone in the room shows respect and helps leave a positive first impression.

Creating a Memorable Conversation

First impressions are often shaped by the quality of the conversation you have with someone. In Kentucky, where people value personal connections, the best way to make a

Resonate, Don't Just Connect:
Fostering Creative, Community-Driven Relationships in Louisville and Kentucky

lasting impact is to have a conversation that is both engaging and meaningful.

1. **Start with Common Ground**: When meeting someone for the first time, it's helpful to find common ground early in the conversation. Whether it's a shared interest in Kentucky's bourbon industry, a mutual connection in the business world, or a passion for horse racing, finding something you both care about can help establish rapport and set a positive tone for the conversation.

2. **Avoid Overly Aggressive Self-Promotion**: While it's important to share what you do and why you're there, avoid turning the conversation into a sales pitch. In Kentucky's business culture, people appreciate humility and authenticity, so focusing too much on promoting yourself can come off as disingenuous. Instead, focus on building a connection first, and the opportunity to discuss your work will naturally follow.

3. **Leave Them with Something to Remember**: One way to ensure that you leave a lasting impression is by leaving the other person with something memorable—whether it's an interesting story, a unique insight, or even a helpful tip. This can help distinguish you from the many other

Resonate, Don't Just Connect:
Fostering Creative, Community-Driven Relationships in Louisville and Kentucky

people they might meet, making it more likely that they'll remember you long after the conversation ends.

Conclusion: Leaving a Lasting Impact in Kentucky

In a state like Kentucky, where personal connections and trust are paramount, first impressions can make or break your success in building meaningful relationships. Whether you're meeting someone in the bourbon industry, agriculture, healthcare, or any of Kentucky's other key sectors, the ability to make a strong and lasting first impression is crucial.

By focusing on preparation, body language, active listening, and genuine sincerity, you can ensure that the first impression you make leaves a positive and lasting impact. In Kentucky, people value relationships built on trust, respect, and authenticity. When you make the effort to be genuine and thoughtful in your interactions, you lay the foundation for long-term connections that can help you succeed in both your personal and professional life.

Resonate, Don't Just Connect:
Fostering Creative, Community-Driven Relationships in Louisville and Kentucky

Chapter 3: Navigating Business Events and Conferences – Tips on Maximizing Value from Industry Gatherings

Business events and conferences provide a unique opportunity to build connections, share knowledge, and expand your network. In a state like Kentucky, where industries such as healthcare, manufacturing, logistics, agriculture, and, of course, bourbon play critical roles in the economy, attending these gatherings can make a significant difference in one's career or business success. Louisville alone hosts numerous national and international conferences each year, thanks to its central location and its thriving sectors, from health and education to equine sports. The challenge for many professionals is not just attending these events but knowing how to navigate them effectively to maximize the value they can bring.

For Kentucky professionals, whether you're attending a regional business expo or a national conference in Louisville or Lexington, learning how to make the most of your time can open doors to new opportunities, partnerships, and insights that could take your career or business to the next level. This chapter will explore

Resonate, Don't Just Connect:
Fostering Creative, Community-Driven Relationships in Louisville and Kentucky

essential strategies for getting the most out of your time at these gatherings, tailored to the specific business and networking culture of Kentucky.

Why Industry Events and Conferences Matter

Before diving into the strategies, it's essential to understand why business events and conferences hold so much value. In Kentucky, many industries are based on personal relationships, and trust is often the deciding factor in business deals or partnerships. This is why face-to-face interactions at events are critical. They allow you to connect on a deeper level, establish trust, and show others that you're not just a name or face behind an email.

Industry gatherings are a chance to build credibility, showcase your knowledge, and learn from others. Whether you're attending a healthcare summit in Louisville or a logistics expo in Bowling Green, you are in an environment where key players, decision-makers, and potential collaborators converge. Kentucky is also a place where family values, authenticity, and long-term relationships matter, so building trust and rapport with fellow professionals at events can significantly impact your career trajectory.

1. Pre-Event Planning

Resonate, Don't Just Connect:
Fostering Creative, Community-Driven Relationships in Louisville and Kentucky

Maximizing the value from a business event or conference starts well before the actual event. The key is to plan ahead and have clear objectives.

Set Clear Goals

Before attending any event, take time to define your goals. Are you looking to meet specific people? Are you trying to gain knowledge in a particular area? Do you want to promote your business or find investors? Having clear objectives ensures that you remain focused throughout the event and use your time efficiently.

For example, at an agricultural expo in Kentucky, your goal might be to learn about the latest sustainable farming practices or to connect with local suppliers. If you're attending a conference focused on healthcare, you might be looking to meet potential partners for your medical tech startup. Whatever your objectives are, defining them helps you navigate the event with purpose.

Research the Event and Attendees

Once you've set your goals, do your homework. Most conferences and business events will provide an agenda, list of speakers, and details about attendees in advance. In Kentucky, where relationships matter, knowing who will be at the event can give you a head start in identifying key people you want to meet. Research the companies and

Resonate, Don't Just Connect:
Fostering Creative, Community-Driven Relationships in Louisville and Kentucky

professionals attending and prioritize those that align with your goals.

For example, if you're attending a bourbon industry conference in Louisville, research the top distilleries and representatives who will be there. This preparation allows you to tailor your approach and have meaningful conversations rather than just general chit-chat. It also shows that you're genuinely interested and informed, which helps make a lasting impression.

Prepare Your Elevator Pitch

An essential part of any business event is introducing yourself in a way that captures attention. In Kentucky, where personal connections and authenticity are highly valued, it's crucial to prepare an elevator pitch that not only tells people what you do but also conveys why you're passionate about it.

Your elevator pitch should be concise and focus on what makes you or your business unique. If you're attending an event like the Kentucky Derby Festival where business owners from all sectors come together, you need a versatile pitch that can appeal to a wide audience. Craft a pitch that reflects your personality and values, as well as the value you can offer to others.

Bring Business Cards and Follow-Up Tools

Resonate, Don't Just Connect:
Fostering Creative, Community-Driven Relationships in Louisville and Kentucky

While business cards might seem old-fashioned, they remain a vital networking tool, especially in Kentucky. People here value face-to-face interactions and personal connections, and exchanging business cards still feels like a personal touch. Ensure that you have enough business cards for everyone you meet and that they clearly reflect your brand or personal identity.

In addition, consider digital follow-up tools like LinkedIn or networking apps to help keep track of new connections. Once you've met someone, it's essential to follow up quickly, so having a system in place for collecting and organizing contacts is crucial.

2. During the Event: Networking Strategies

Once you've prepared for the event, the next step is navigating the actual event or conference itself. Here are key strategies to maximize your value while attending.

Be Intentional with Your Time

It's easy to become overwhelmed at large events, especially ones like the Kentucky Bourbon Festival or the Kentucky Manufacturing Conference, where there are dozens of sessions, speakers, and exhibitors. Prioritize the sessions and people that align with your goals and make a plan. If possible, schedule meetings with key contacts in advance. Use the agenda to map out the sessions you want

Resonate, Don't Just Connect:
Fostering Creative, Community-Driven Relationships in Louisville and Kentucky

to attend, leaving enough room for networking in between.

It's also helpful to avoid spending too much time with people you already know. Conferences are about expanding your network, not just catching up with familiar faces. Focus on meeting new people who can bring fresh insights or opportunities to your career or business.

Ask Thoughtful Questions

At any event, but particularly in Kentucky, where authenticity is valued, asking thoughtful questions can help you stand out. Whether you're attending a panel discussion or meeting someone at a networking session, asking questions that show genuine curiosity and interest in the other person's work goes a long way.

For example, if you're at a healthcare summit in Lexington, ask speakers or attendees how they see the future of healthcare evolving in Kentucky and what role local companies might play. People appreciate when you're engaged in a meaningful way, and it helps foster deeper connections beyond surface-level small talk.

Build Relationships, Not Just Contacts

Networking events can often feel transactional, where people are only interested in what they can gain from each other. However, in Kentucky's business culture, building

Resonate, Don't Just Connect:
Fostering Creative, Community-Driven Relationships in Louisville and Kentucky

long-term relationships is far more valuable than simply collecting business cards. Take the time to get to know people personally. Show interest in their stories, and offer value wherever you can.

For instance, if you meet someone from a distillery at a bourbon industry event, don't immediately jump to what they can do for you. Instead, ask about their journey in the industry, what challenges they're facing, and how you might help them. By focusing on building genuine connections, you'll create relationships that last far beyond the event itself.

Be Approachable and Confident

Conferences can be intimidating, especially if you're new to the event or don't know anyone. However, one of the keys to successful networking is being approachable and confident. This doesn't mean being overly aggressive, but rather presenting yourself in a way that invites conversation.

Smile, make eye contact, and be open to talking to new people. Confidence is contagious, and when you exude it, others will naturally be drawn to you. In Kentucky, where hospitality is a core value, people appreciate a warm and approachable demeanor. This can help set you apart and create a positive first impression.

Utilize Breaks and Social Events

Resonate, Don't Just Connect:
Fostering Creative, Community-Driven Relationships in Louisville and Kentucky

Many of the most valuable connections at conferences don't happen in the formal sessions but during breaks and social events. Whether it's a coffee break between panels, a cocktail hour, or a networking dinner, these informal settings are where real relationships are often built.

In Kentucky, where business and social life often intertwine, attending social events is just as important as the sessions themselves. These gatherings provide a more relaxed environment where you can connect with others on a personal level, share stories, and establish rapport. Be sure to attend these events and engage with people beyond just discussing business.

Participate Actively in Discussions

If the event involves panel discussions or Q&A sessions, don't be afraid to participate actively. Asking insightful questions during these moments can help you stand out and showcase your knowledge. It also signals to others that you're engaged and interested in the topic, which can open the door for conversations afterward.

For instance, if you're at a logistics conference in Bowling Green, asking a thoughtful question about how Kentucky's central location influences global shipping trends can demonstrate your understanding of the local industry and help position you as a thought leader in the space.

Resonate, Don't Just Connect:
Fostering Creative, Community-Driven Relationships in Louisville and Kentucky

3. Post-Event Follow-Up

Your work doesn't end when the event is over. In fact, the follow-up process is one of the most critical components of maximizing value from conferences and events. This is where you solidify the connections you made and turn them into actionable relationships.

Follow Up Quickly

After meeting new contacts at an event, follow up within 24 to 48 hours. This ensures that you remain fresh in their mind and shows that you are serious about maintaining the relationship. Whether it's a quick thank-you email, a LinkedIn connection, or even a phone call, following up promptly is essential.

In your follow-up message, reference something specific from your conversation to show that you were paying attention. For example, if you met someone at a manufacturing expo and discussed automation trends, mention that in your email to make it more personal and memorable.

Offer Value in Your Follow-Up

When following up with a new connection, it's important not to ask for favors right away. Instead, offer value in your follow-up. This could be something as simple as sharing a relevant article, introducing them to someone in

Resonate, Don't Just Connect:
Fostering Creative, Community-Driven Relationships in Louisville and Kentucky

your network, or providing a resource that could help their business.

By focusing on giving rather than taking, you'll position yourself as someone who genuinely wants to build a mutually beneficial relationship. In Kentucky, where long-term trust is highly valued, this approach will help strengthen the connection.

Stay Connected

Building a relationship doesn't end after the first follow-up. Continue to stay connected with your new contacts by periodically checking in, sharing updates, or inviting them to future events. In Kentucky, where the business community is often closely connected, maintaining relationships over time can lead to new opportunities and collaborations down the road.

For example, if you meet someone at a healthcare summit, you might follow up a few months later to ask how a project they mentioned is going or to invite them to another relevant event. This keeps the relationship alive and positions you as someone who is genuinely interested in their success.

4. Leveraging Kentucky's Unique Business Events

Kentucky is home to numerous business events and conferences that provide invaluable opportunities for networking and industry growth. Knowing how to

Resonate, Don't Just Connect:
Fostering Creative, Community-Driven Relationships in Louisville and Kentucky

navigate these events in the context of Kentucky's unique industries can help you make the most of your time.

Bourbon Industry Events

The bourbon industry is a cornerstone of Kentucky's economy, and events like the Kentucky Bourbon Festival provide an excellent platform for networking. When attending bourbon-related events, it's important to understand the history and culture of bourbon in the state. Whether you're in the industry or just interested in learning more, showing respect for the tradition and knowledge of bourbon will help you connect with industry professionals.

Healthcare Conferences

Louisville is home to some of the largest healthcare companies in the nation, and conferences in this sector provide ample opportunity to meet industry leaders. When attending healthcare events, focus on discussing emerging trends like telemedicine, healthcare technology, and patient-centered care—topics that are top of mind for Kentucky's healthcare professionals.

Manufacturing and Logistics Expos

Kentucky's central location makes it a hub for manufacturing and logistics, with companies like UPS and Toyota having a significant presence in the state. Attending these expos provides a chance to connect with

Resonate, Don't Just Connect:
Fostering Creative, Community-Driven Relationships in Louisville and Kentucky

leaders in these industries. When navigating manufacturing and logistics events, focus on conversations about automation, supply chain optimization, and workforce development—key issues that are shaping the future of these sectors in Kentucky.

Conclusion: Making the Most of Kentucky's Business Events and Conferences

Navigating business events and conferences in Kentucky requires preparation, intentionality, and the ability to build genuine relationships. Whether you're attending a small industry gathering or a large international conference in Louisville, the strategies outlined in this chapter will help you maximize the value of your time and create lasting connections.

In Kentucky, where trust, authenticity, and long-term relationships are paramount, approaching business events with the right mindset can lead to new opportunities and long-term success. By preparing in advance, engaging meaningfully with others, and following up effectively, you can unlock the full potential of every event you attend and build a network that supports your growth for years to come.

Resonate, Don't Just Connect:
Fostering Creative, Community-Driven Relationships in Louisville and Kentucky

Chapter 4: The Follow-Up Formula – How to Maintain and Nurture Relationships Long After the First Meeting

In the world of business and networking, first impressions are only the beginning. Building a meaningful, long-term relationship requires consistent effort, especially after that initial meeting. In Kentucky, where relationships are often built on trust, loyalty, and mutual respect, the follow-up process is crucial to maintaining and nurturing the connections you make at business events, conferences, or even casual meetings.

Kentucky's business culture, rooted in hospitality, community values, and a strong work ethic, places a high value on relationships that stand the test of time. Whether you're doing business in Louisville, Lexington, or rural Kentucky, maintaining relationships is the foundation for success. The way you follow up after a meeting can significantly influence how people perceive you and how the relationship progresses over time.

This chapter will explore the "Follow-Up Formula" — a strategic approach to keeping the momentum going after the first meeting. It will focus on how to stay top of mind,

Resonate, Don't Just Connect:
Fostering Creative, Community-Driven Relationships in Louisville and Kentucky

offer value, and build trust, particularly in the context of Kentucky's unique business landscape.

1. Why Follow-Up Matters

In Kentucky, where businesses and industries are often interconnected and tightly knit, failing to follow up can lead to missed opportunities. It's not uncommon for people to form opinions based on your ability to keep promises and stay in touch. While the initial meeting or introduction is important, the real relationship-building begins after that first interaction.

Following up shows that you're serious about the connection and that you value the other person's time. It also helps reinforce the positive impression you made during the first meeting. Whether you're trying to cultivate a business partnership, land a new client, or simply expand your professional network, the follow-up is where you prove your reliability and build trust over time.

The Kentucky Factor: Relationship-Centric Culture

In a state like Kentucky, where people often rely on word-of-mouth recommendations and long-standing relationships, following up is not just about politeness; it's a way of building lasting business and personal connections. People here value integrity and consistency, and those who can nurture relationships through

Resonate, Don't Just Connect:
Fostering Creative, Community-Driven Relationships in Louisville and Kentucky

consistent and meaningful follow-up are more likely to succeed in the long run.

The follow-up process in Kentucky's business environment often extends beyond email and LinkedIn messages. It can include face-to-face meetings, attending events together, or supporting local initiatives. The more you integrate yourself into the community, the stronger your relationships will become.

2. Timing Your Follow-Up

One of the key aspects of a successful follow-up is timing. If you wait too long, the other person may forget who you are or lose interest. On the other hand, following up too quickly or too frequently can come off as pushy. The trick is to strike the right balance and stay relevant without overwhelming the other person.

Immediate Follow-Up (Within 24-48 Hours)

The first step in the follow-up formula is to reach out within 24 to 48 hours after your initial meeting. This quick follow-up serves as a reminder of your interaction and helps reinforce the positive impression you made. It's also an opportunity to express gratitude for the person's time and reiterate any key points from your conversation.

In Kentucky, where personal relationships matter, this initial follow-up can be more than just a polite gesture — it's a way of demonstrating your sincerity and

Resonate, Don't Just Connect:
Fostering Creative, Community-Driven Relationships in Louisville and Kentucky

professionalism. Whether it's a quick email, a handwritten note, or a LinkedIn message, this first follow-up sets the tone for the relationship moving forward.

For example, if you met someone at a healthcare conference in Louisville, your follow-up message might look something like this:

"Hi [Name],
It was great meeting you at the [Event Name]! I really enjoyed our conversation about healthcare innovation and Kentucky's role in the future of telemedicine. I'd love to stay in touch and explore ways we can collaborate or share ideas. Please feel free to reach out if there's anything I can assist with.
Best,
[Your Name]"

This message is simple, polite, and reinforces the connection without being overbearing. The goal is to keep the conversation going in a natural way.

Medium-Term Follow-Up (Within 1-2 Weeks)

Once you've sent the immediate follow-up, it's important to keep the relationship alive by checking in again within a week or two. This is especially important if your initial conversation involved potential business deals, partnerships, or collaboration opportunities. The medium-term follow-up allows you to build on the foundation

Resonate, Don't Just Connect:
Fostering Creative, Community-Driven Relationships in Louisville and Kentucky

you've established and keep the relationship moving forward.

At this stage, you might offer additional value, such as sharing a relevant article, introducing the person to someone in your network, or offering to meet for coffee or a follow-up meeting. The key is to remain helpful and engaged without being too aggressive.

For example, if you're in the logistics industry and met someone at a business expo in Bowling Green, your follow-up might look like this:

"Hi [Name],
I hope you're doing well. I came across this article about supply chain optimization in Kentucky and thought it might interest you based on our conversation at [Event Name]. If you're free sometime next week, I'd love to grab coffee and continue our discussion on how we can tackle some of the challenges facing the logistics industry. Let me know what works for you!
Best regards,
[Your Name]"

This message offers value by sharing relevant information while also suggesting a next step. The focus remains on the other person and how you can continue to build the relationship.

Long-Term Follow-Up (Ongoing)

Resonate, Don't Just Connect:
Fostering Creative, Community-Driven Relationships in Louisville and Kentucky

Building long-term relationships requires ongoing effort. After your initial follow-ups, you should stay in touch periodically to maintain the connection. This can be done through a variety of methods, such as attending industry events together, checking in via email, or even sending holiday greetings.

In Kentucky's business culture, where community and relationships are often intertwined, attending local events, supporting community initiatives, or simply being present at important functions can go a long way in nurturing relationships. Long-term follow-up isn't about constantly asking for favors or pushing your agenda. Instead, it's about showing that you're invested in the relationship and genuinely care about the other person's success.

3. Offering Value in Your Follow-Up

One of the most important elements of any follow-up is offering value. This is especially true in Kentucky, where people appreciate when you contribute to their success, rather than just seeking something for yourself. When you follow up, think about how you can help the other person, whether that's through providing information, introducing them to someone in your network, or offering your expertise.

Share Relevant Information

Resonate, Don't Just Connect:
Fostering Creative, Community-Driven Relationships in Louisville and Kentucky

One simple way to offer value in your follow-up is by sharing information that's relevant to the person's business or industry. This could be an article, a report, or a piece of news that relates to your previous conversation. Sharing relevant information not only keeps the conversation going but also demonstrates that you're paying attention and that you care about their interests.

For instance, if you met someone at a bourbon industry event in Louisville, you might follow up by sending them a recent article on bourbon trends or legislation affecting the industry. This small gesture shows that you're staying informed and are genuinely interested in their work.

Make Introductions

Another effective way to offer value is by making introductions. If you know someone who could be beneficial to the person you met, offering to introduce them can help strengthen your relationship and provide value to both parties. In Kentucky, where networking is often based on personal relationships and referrals, making a meaningful introduction can go a long way in building trust.

For example, if you met someone at a manufacturing expo in Lexington and know a potential client or partner for their business, you might say:

Resonate, Don't Just Connect:
Fostering Creative, Community-Driven Relationships in Louisville and Kentucky

"Hi [Name],

I was thinking about our conversation at [Event Name] and realized that you might benefit from connecting with [Person's Name], who runs a [business description]. I'd be happy to introduce you both if you're interested. Let me know if that sounds helpful!

Best,

[Your Name]"

This message shows that you're thinking about how you can help them succeed and are willing to leverage your network to do so.

Offer Your Expertise

Offering your expertise or services without expecting anything in return is another powerful way to add value in your follow-up. If you have skills, knowledge, or resources that could benefit the person you met, don't hesitate to offer them.

For example, if you're an expert in digital marketing and met a small business owner at a Kentucky business summit, you might offer to help them with a specific marketing challenge they're facing. Offering your expertise for free or at a discounted rate can create goodwill and strengthen the relationship.

4. Building Trust Through Consistency

Resonate, Don't Just Connect:
Fostering Creative, Community-Driven Relationships in Louisville and Kentucky

In Kentucky's business culture, trust is one of the most valuable commodities. Building and maintaining trust requires consistency over time. Following up isn't just about staying in touch — it's about proving that you're reliable and trustworthy. The more consistent you are in your follow-ups, the more trust you build.

Be Reliable

If you promise to follow up after a meeting, make sure you do so. If you say you'll send an article or make an introduction, follow through promptly. Inconsistent or unreliable follow-up can damage your reputation and make it harder to build meaningful relationships.

In Kentucky, where reputation plays a significant role in business, being known as someone who keeps their word is essential. The follow-up process is an opportunity to demonstrate that you're dependable, which is a critical factor in building trust.

Stay Visible

Maintaining visibility is another important aspect of consistent follow-up. This doesn't mean bombarding the other person with constant messages, but rather finding ways to stay top of mind in a positive and helpful way.

For instance, you can attend industry events or local community gatherings where the person is likely to be present. If you're involved in the same business circles,

Resonate, Don't Just Connect:
Fostering Creative, Community-Driven Relationships in Louisville and Kentucky

simply showing up regularly can help reinforce your presence and keep the relationship strong.

In Kentucky, where business and social life often intersect, staying visible in the community can help maintain relationships without the need for constant direct communication.

Keep It Personal

As you nurture your relationships over time, it's important to keep your follow-ups personal and tailored to the individual. Generic or mass emails won't have the same impact as a personalized message that references your previous conversations or shared experiences.

In Kentucky's business culture, where people value personal connections, taking the time to send a personalized note shows that you care about the relationship and are invested in maintaining it. Whether it's a simple check-in or a congratulatory message for a recent achievement, keeping things personal helps build stronger connections.

5. Navigating Challenges in the Follow-Up Process

While the follow-up process is essential for building long-term relationships, it's not always smooth sailing. You may encounter challenges along the way, such as unresponsive contacts, or difficulty finding ways to add

Resonate, Don't Just Connect:
Fostering Creative, Community-Driven Relationships in Louisville and Kentucky

value. Navigating these challenges effectively can help ensure that your follow-up efforts are successful.

Dealing with Unresponsive Contacts

Not everyone will respond to your follow-up messages right away, and that's okay. It's important to be patient and persistent without being pushy. If you don't hear back from someone after your initial follow-up, give it some time before reaching out again.

In Kentucky, where people often juggle multiple commitments, it's not uncommon for busy professionals to take longer to respond. Give them the benefit of the doubt and send a polite follow-up after a reasonable amount of time, such as a week or two.

Finding New Ways to Add Value

If you find that you've run out of ways to offer value in your follow-up, take the time to reassess the relationship and look for new opportunities. For instance, you might explore their industry trends or challenges and find ways to help them navigate those issues.

In Kentucky's business environment, where industries like agriculture, healthcare, and manufacturing are constantly evolving, staying informed about the latest developments can help you offer relevant value in your follow-ups.

Resonate, Don't Just Connect:
Fostering Creative, Community-Driven Relationships in Louisville and Kentucky

6. Turning Follow-Up Into Long-Term Partnerships

Ultimately, the goal of follow-up is to turn initial meetings and connections into long-term partnerships. By staying consistent, offering value, and building trust, you can cultivate relationships that lead to new business opportunities, collaborations, and friendships.

In Kentucky, where community and relationships are at the heart of business success, long-term partnerships are often built on the foundation of consistent follow-up and mutual respect. By following the steps outlined in this chapter, you can develop a follow-up strategy that not only keeps you top of mind but also helps you build meaningful, lasting relationships.

Conclusion: The Follow-Up Formula in Kentucky

Navigating the follow-up process is essential for building strong, long-term relationships in Kentucky's business community. By focusing on timing, offering value, building trust, and staying consistent, you can turn initial meetings into lasting connections that drive success for years to come.

In Kentucky, where relationships are often the key to business success, mastering the art of follow-up can set you apart and help you build a network of trusted partners, clients, and collaborators. Whether you're attending a local business event or a national conference,

Resonate, Don't Just Connect:
Fostering Creative, Community-Driven Relationships in Louisville and Kentucky

the Follow-Up Formula will help you nurture and grow the relationships that matter most.

Resonate, Don't Just Connect:
Fostering Creative, Community-Driven Relationships in Louisville and Kentucky

Chapter 5: Networking in the Digital Age – Utilizing Platforms Like LinkedIn and Social Media to Expand Your Circle

The rise of digital networking platforms has revolutionized the way we connect with others, making it easier than ever to expand our professional circles, share knowledge, and collaborate across industries and geographies. In Kentucky, a state that blends tradition with innovation, digital networking offers a unique opportunity to connect local industries—such as bourbon, agriculture, manufacturing, and healthcare—with global trends and communities. Whether you're in Louisville, Lexington, or a more rural part of the state, understanding how to leverage platforms like LinkedIn and other social media channels is essential for growing your network, building meaningful relationships, and staying ahead in today's rapidly changing business environment.

In Kentucky, a state known for its tight-knit communities and strong business relationships, digital networking platforms don't replace face-to-face interactions but rather complement them. These tools allow professionals to stay connected, share resources, and cultivate relationships long after in-person meetings have ended. This chapter

Resonate, Don't Just Connect:
Fostering Creative, Community-Driven Relationships in Louisville and Kentucky

will explore how you can harness the power of LinkedIn, other social media platforms, and digital networking strategies to expand your professional network in Kentucky and beyond.

The Digital Transformation of Networking

In the past, professional networking was largely confined to in-person events, conferences, and chance meetings. While these face-to-face interactions remain valuable, the digital age has dramatically expanded the possibilities for connecting with others. Platforms like LinkedIn, Twitter, Instagram, and even Facebook have transformed networking into an ongoing process that can happen anytime, anywhere.

In Kentucky, a state with industries that are deeply rooted in local communities, this digital transformation has allowed businesses and professionals to expand their reach far beyond state lines. Whether you're a healthcare professional in Lexington, a bourbon distiller in Louisville, or a farmer in the rural Bluegrass region, digital networking enables you to connect with industry leaders, potential clients, and collaborators across the globe.

Digital networking allows you to:

- Connect with professionals across industries and geographies.

Resonate, Don't Just Connect:
Fostering Creative, Community-Driven Relationships in Louisville and Kentucky

- Share and consume content that builds your personal and professional brand.
- Stay updated on industry trends and innovations.
- Collaborate in real-time, regardless of location.
- Build and nurture relationships with ease, using tools that make it simple to follow up, stay in touch, and provide value.

Kentucky's blend of traditional industries and growing tech sectors makes it the perfect state to embrace the potential of digital networking. But to fully leverage these tools, you need to understand how to use them effectively, starting with the most powerful professional networking platform: LinkedIn.

1. Leveraging LinkedIn for Professional Networking

LinkedIn is widely recognized as the premier platform for professional networking. With more than 900 million users globally, it offers a unique space to connect with like-minded professionals, share industry insights, and showcase your expertise. For professionals in Kentucky, LinkedIn serves as a bridge between the state's strong local business community and the broader global network.

Optimizing Your LinkedIn Profile

The first step to making the most of LinkedIn is to optimize your profile. Your LinkedIn profile acts as your

Resonate, Don't Just Connect:
Fostering Creative, Community-Driven Relationships in Louisville and Kentucky

digital business card, résumé, and portfolio all in one. For Kentucky professionals, whether you're in logistics, healthcare, education, or agriculture, a well-crafted LinkedIn profile can help you stand out and make a positive first impression.

Key elements to focus on include:

- **Profile Photo**: A professional headshot is essential for making a strong first impression. In Kentucky's business culture, where relationships are often built on trust, having a clear, approachable, and professional photo helps establish credibility.

- **Headline**: Your headline should clearly communicate who you are and what you do. Instead of simply listing your job title, consider framing it in a way that highlights your unique value proposition. For example, "Helping Kentucky's Bourbon Industry Thrive Through Innovative Logistics Solutions" is more engaging than "Logistics Manager."

- **About Section**: This is your chance to tell your professional story. Be sure to mention key accomplishments, your areas of expertise, and how you add value to your industry. Kentucky professionals can also highlight their ties to the

Resonate, Don't Just Connect:
Fostering Creative, Community-Driven Relationships in Louisville and Kentucky

state's industries, culture, and values, which can resonate with both local and global audiences.

- **Experience and Skills**: Make sure your experience is up to date, and include detailed descriptions of your roles, accomplishments, and impact. List relevant skills, and request endorsements from colleagues to boost your credibility.

In Kentucky, where many industries are deeply traditional—such as agriculture, bourbon, and manufacturing—combining your local experience with a digital presence on LinkedIn can showcase your ability to bridge the gap between traditional and modern business practices.

Connecting with the Right People

LinkedIn makes it easy to connect with professionals from all walks of life, but it's important to be intentional about who you connect with. While it might be tempting to accept every connection request, a focused and curated network will provide more value.

Start by connecting with people you've met in person at Kentucky business events, conferences, or through mutual acquaintances. Then, expand your network by connecting with industry leaders, thought leaders, and peers in your field. When sending a connection request, always include

Resonate, Don't Just Connect:
Fostering Creative, Community-Driven Relationships in Louisville and Kentucky

a personalized message. A brief introduction or reminder of how you met helps establish a personal connection.

For example:

"Hi [Name],
It was great meeting you at the Kentucky Manufacturing Expo last week. I enjoyed our conversation about the role of automation in local industries. I'd love to stay connected and continue the conversation!
Best regards,
[Your Name]"

In Kentucky, where face-to-face interactions still play a large role in business, following up with a digital connection on LinkedIn after meeting someone in person is a great way to maintain the relationship and keep the conversation going.

Sharing Valuable Content

One of LinkedIn's most powerful features is its ability to serve as a content-sharing platform. By sharing valuable content—whether it's industry articles, personal insights, or updates on your business—you can position yourself as a thought leader and keep your network engaged.

Kentucky professionals can share content that's relevant to the state's key industries, such as healthcare, logistics, agriculture, or bourbon production. Sharing local news or commenting on statewide economic trends can help

Resonate, Don't Just Connect:
Fostering Creative, Community-Driven Relationships in Louisville and Kentucky

demonstrate your engagement with Kentucky's business community, while also highlighting your expertise to a broader audience.

Consider posting:

- **Industry Insights**: Share articles, case studies, or reports related to your field. Add your own commentary to show your perspective and expertise.

- **Company Updates**: Share updates on what's happening at your company, whether it's a new project, a community initiative, or a successful client story.

- **Local Events**: Promote or comment on upcoming events, conferences, or business expos in Kentucky. This can help you stay visible in the local business community and encourage face-to-face interactions.

For example, a healthcare professional in Lexington might share an article about telemedicine trends and add their own thoughts on how Kentucky healthcare providers are adapting to digital healthcare solutions.

Engaging with Your Network

Networking on LinkedIn is not just about connecting with others—it's about engaging with them. This means liking,

Resonate, Don't Just Connect:
Fostering Creative, Community-Driven Relationships in Louisville and Kentucky

commenting on, and sharing others' posts. Kentucky is known for its sense of community, and building a supportive, engaged network online can reflect the values of collaboration and mutual support that the state is known for.

Take the time to engage meaningfully with others' content. If a colleague shares an article, leave a thoughtful comment. If someone in your network announces a new job, congratulate them. These small actions help keep you visible in your network and build stronger relationships over time.

For instance, if someone in your network posts about the growing importance of sustainable farming in Kentucky, you might comment with, "Great post! Sustainability is such a critical issue for Kentucky's agricultural future. Looking forward to seeing how local farmers and innovators continue to lead the way."

2. Using Twitter for Thought Leadership and Industry Updates

While LinkedIn is the go-to platform for professional networking, Twitter also plays an important role in digital networking, especially for professionals who want to position themselves as thought leaders or stay updated on industry trends.

Following Industry Leaders and Hashtags

Resonate, Don't Just Connect:
Fostering Creative, Community-Driven Relationships in Louisville and Kentucky

Twitter allows you to follow key industry leaders, businesses, and organizations, making it easy to stay up to date on the latest trends. For Kentucky professionals, this could mean following local companies like Yum! Brands or Humana, as well as national and global thought leaders in your field.

In addition to following individual accounts, tracking relevant hashtags can help you stay informed. For example, hashtags like #KYBourbon, #KentuckyHealthcare, or #KYAg (for agriculture) are commonly used in Kentucky's business community. By keeping an eye on these hashtags, you can engage in conversations that are relevant to your industry and geography.

Tweeting and Engaging in Conversations

Tweeting your own insights or sharing industry news can help you build a following and position yourself as a knowledgeable professional in your field. Keep your tweets concise and informative, and be sure to engage with others by replying to their tweets, retweeting valuable content, and participating in conversations.

For example, a logistics professional in Louisville might tweet about how Kentucky's central location positions the state as a key player in the national supply chain:

Resonate, Don't Just Connect:
Fostering Creative, Community-Driven Relationships in Louisville and Kentucky

"With Louisville's UPS hub and Kentucky's strategic location, our state plays a critical role in the national supply chain. Excited to see how new tech innovations will enhance efficiency. #KYLogistics #SupplyChainInnovation"

By using relevant hashtags and engaging with industry peers, you can expand your reach and build connections with people who share your interests.

Participating in Twitter Chats

Twitter chats are scheduled discussions that revolve around specific topics and use designated hashtags. Participating in these chats can be a great way to connect with industry leaders and peers in real-time, share your expertise, and expand your network.

For Kentucky professionals, there may be local or industry-specific Twitter chats focused on topics like bourbon production, healthcare innovation, or sustainable farming. Participating in these discussions not only helps you stay informed but also allows you to contribute your own insights, positioning yourself as an active member of the professional community.

3. Facebook, Instagram, and Niche Platforms

While LinkedIn and Twitter are the most commonly used platforms for professional networking, other social media

Resonate, Don't Just Connect:
Fostering Creative, Community-Driven Relationships in Louisville and Kentucky

platforms like Facebook and Instagram can also play a role, especially for certain industries.

Facebook for Local Business and Community Engagement

Facebook is particularly useful for engaging with local businesses and communities. Many local business groups, chambers of commerce, and industry organizations in Kentucky maintain active Facebook pages or groups where members can share news, events, and resources.

For example, you might join a Facebook group for small business owners in Kentucky, where you can network with other local entrepreneurs, share advice, and learn about upcoming events. Facebook can also be a valuable platform for staying connected with local communities and showing support for local initiatives, which can help strengthen your personal brand and build goodwill.

Instagram for Visual Industries

Instagram is a highly visual platform, making it especially valuable for professionals in industries like fashion, beauty, design, or food and beverage. For Kentucky's bourbon industry, for example, Instagram offers an opportunity to showcase the craftsmanship, heritage, and aesthetic appeal of bourbon production.

If you're in a visual industry, using Instagram to post high-quality images of your work, behind-the-scenes

Resonate, Don't Just Connect:
Fostering Creative, Community-Driven Relationships in Louisville and Kentucky

shots, or industry events can help you build a following and engage with both local and global audiences. For Kentucky businesses that rely on aesthetics, Instagram is a powerful tool for storytelling and brand building.

Niche Platforms and Industry-Specific Networks

Depending on your industry, there may be niche platforms that offer additional networking opportunities. For example, Behance is a platform for creatives to showcase their work, while ResearchGate is a network for academics and researchers to share their publications. In Kentucky's healthcare industry, platforms like Doximity allow doctors and medical professionals to network and share research.

For professionals in Kentucky's specialized industries, exploring these niche platforms can provide opportunities to connect with others who share your expertise and interests.

4. Integrating Digital and Face-to-Face Networking

While digital networking platforms are powerful tools, they work best when integrated with face-to-face interactions. In Kentucky, where business relationships are often built on personal trust and community involvement, combining digital and in-person networking can help you build stronger, more meaningful connections.

Resonate, Don't Just Connect:
Fostering Creative, Community-Driven Relationships in Louisville and Kentucky

Attend Local Events and Follow Up Online

Whenever you attend a local business event, conference, or industry gathering in Kentucky, be sure to follow up with the people you meet on LinkedIn or other social media platforms. This not only reinforces the connection but also provides a way to stay in touch over the long term.

For example, after attending the Kentucky Derby or a local healthcare summit, you might follow up with the people you met by sending a LinkedIn connection request or tagging them in a post about the event. This helps bridge the gap between in-person and online networking, keeping the relationship alive.

Use Digital Tools to Stay in Touch

Digital networking platforms make it easier to stay in touch with people even after the initial meeting. Take advantage of these tools by periodically engaging with your contacts—whether that means liking their LinkedIn posts, sending them a message to check in, or inviting them to future events.

In Kentucky's business community, where relationships often span years, maintaining regular contact is key to building long-term connections. Digital tools provide an easy way to keep the conversation going and ensure that you stay top of mind.

Resonate, Don't Just Connect:
Fostering Creative, Community-Driven Relationships in Louisville and Kentucky

5. Building a Personal Brand Online

One of the greatest advantages of digital networking is the ability to build a personal brand that reflects your expertise, values, and professional goals. In Kentucky, where industries like bourbon, healthcare, and logistics are closely tied to the state's identity, your personal brand can reflect both your professional skills and your connection to Kentucky's culture and industries.

Consistency Is Key

When building your personal brand online, consistency is key. This means using the same professional photo, tone of voice, and messaging across all your platforms—whether you're on LinkedIn, Twitter, Instagram, or Facebook. A consistent brand helps people recognize you and understand what you stand for.

Share Your Values

In Kentucky, where community values like trust, integrity, and hospitality are central to the business culture, sharing your personal values online can help differentiate you and build trust with your network. Whether you're posting about local business initiatives, commenting on industry trends, or sharing updates about your own work, make sure your values come through in your content.

Resonate, Don't Just Connect:
Fostering Creative, Community-Driven Relationships in Louisville and Kentucky

For example, if you're passionate about sustainable farming in Kentucky, make that a central theme of your online presence by sharing articles, engaging in discussions, and showcasing your involvement in local initiatives.

Be Authentic

Authenticity is crucial when building a personal brand. In Kentucky, where business relationships are often built on personal trust, being genuine and transparent online will help you build stronger connections. Don't be afraid to share personal stories, lessons learned, or challenges you've overcome in your professional journey. Authenticity helps build rapport and fosters deeper relationships, both online and offline.

Conclusion: Expanding Your Network in the Digital Age

Networking in the digital age offers endless opportunities for Kentucky professionals to expand their circles, build meaningful relationships, and grow their careers. By leveraging platforms like LinkedIn, Twitter, Instagram, and even niche networks, you can connect with industry leaders, collaborate with peers, and stay updated on the latest trends—both locally and globally.

In Kentucky, where business is often rooted in tradition and community, digital networking serves as a powerful

Resonate, Don't Just Connect:
Fostering Creative, Community-Driven Relationships in Louisville and Kentucky

complement to face-to-face interactions. By integrating online and offline networking strategies, building a strong personal brand, and consistently offering value to your network, you can cultivate relationships that stand the test of time and contribute to your long-term success.

As Kentucky continues to grow and evolve in industries like healthcare, bourbon, logistics, and agriculture, professionals who embrace digital networking will be well-positioned to thrive in this dynamic business landscape.

Resonate, Don't Just Connect:
Fostering Creative, Community-Driven Relationships in Louisville and Kentucky

Chapter 6: Leveraging Your Network for Business Growth – Turning Connections into Opportunities

In Kentucky, a state deeply rooted in community, trust, and relationships, leveraging your professional network is more than just a business strategy; it's a cultural imperative. The strong sense of collaboration and community that defines Kentucky's industries—from bourbon distilleries and equine businesses to healthcare and logistics—makes the ability to turn connections into opportunities a key factor for success.

Whether you are in Louisville, Lexington, or a rural part of the state, your network can serve as the engine that drives business growth, offering pathways to partnerships, customer acquisition, investments, and innovation. However, leveraging your network requires more than simply having a long list of contacts. It's about fostering relationships that create mutual value, strategically engaging with the right people, and taking consistent action to convert those connections into tangible business opportunities.

In this chapter, we will explore strategies for turning your professional network into a powerful tool for business

Resonate, Don't Just Connect:
Fostering Creative, Community-Driven Relationships in Louisville and Kentucky

growth, with a special focus on Kentucky's business environment. We'll cover how to identify and cultivate high-value connections, the importance of reciprocity in business relationships, and actionable tactics for converting those connections into opportunities for growth.

1. Understanding the Value of Your Network

Before diving into specific strategies, it's important to understand the value that your network brings to the table. In Kentucky, where industries are often interconnected and reputation carries significant weight, your network can provide access to a variety of opportunities that might otherwise be out of reach. Whether you're in the bourbon industry in Louisville, the logistics hub of Northern Kentucky, or the healthcare sector in Lexington, leveraging relationships can open doors to partnerships, resources, and customers that are critical to growing your business.

The Kentucky Business Landscape

Kentucky's diverse economy is home to several key industries that thrive on relationships, such as bourbon, equine sports, healthcare, logistics, and manufacturing. In each of these sectors, personal connections are often the foundation for success. For instance, in the bourbon industry, many business deals and partnerships are built on long-standing relationships between distilleries,

Resonate, Don't Just Connect:
Fostering Creative, Community-Driven Relationships in Louisville and Kentucky

suppliers, and distributors. Similarly, in the healthcare sector, collaborations between hospitals, tech startups, and medical professionals are often facilitated through trusted networks.

Understanding this interconnected landscape is crucial for leveraging your network effectively. Building strong relationships in Kentucky's business community can lead to opportunities that range from new clients and partnerships to investments and strategic alliances. However, the key to unlocking these opportunities lies in knowing how to nurture and expand your network.

Assessing Your Current Network

Before you can begin leveraging your network for growth, it's important to assess where you stand. Take a moment to evaluate your current connections and identify those that have the potential to contribute to your business growth. This doesn't just mean high-level executives or influential figures; it includes anyone who has knowledge, skills, or relationships that could benefit your business.

Consider the following:

- **Industry Relevance**: Do you have connections within your industry who can help you navigate the local market, introduce you to potential clients, or provide industry insights?

Resonate, Don't Just Connect:
Fostering Creative, Community-Driven Relationships in Louisville and Kentucky

- **Geographical Reach**: Do you have contacts who can help you expand beyond your local region into other parts of Kentucky or even nationally?

- **Influence and Decision-Making Power**: Are there people in your network who hold influence within their organizations or industries? These individuals can be pivotal in helping you access new opportunities.

- **Diversity of Skills and Expertise**: A well-rounded network should include people with diverse skills and expertise. This could include marketing experts, financial advisors, or supply chain specialists who can offer different perspectives and support your business growth.

Once you have a clear understanding of your existing network, you can begin identifying gaps and areas for expansion.

2. Building High-Value Connections

Leveraging your network for business growth requires more than just having a large number of connections; it's about having the right connections. High-value connections are those that align with your business goals, offer expertise or resources, and are willing to collaborate on mutually beneficial opportunities. Building these relationships takes time, effort, and intentionality.

Resonate, Don't Just Connect:
Fostering Creative, Community-Driven Relationships in Louisville and Kentucky

Identify Key Influencers and Connectors

In Kentucky's business environment, key influencers and connectors can make a significant impact on your ability to grow. These are individuals who not only hold influence within their industries but also have extensive networks themselves. They are often the ones who can introduce you to new opportunities, open doors to high-level partnerships, or connect you with valuable resources.

In industries like healthcare or bourbon, for example, connecting with leaders or seasoned professionals who have built successful careers can offer insights and introductions that are critical for your growth. These influencers often attend industry events, conferences, and community gatherings, so it's important to be present at these opportunities to engage with them.

To identify key influencers and connectors in Kentucky, consider the following:

- **Industry Events and Conferences**: Events like the Kentucky Bourbon Festival, the Lexington Healthcare Summit, or the Kentucky Manufacturing Expo are ideal places to meet industry leaders and build relationships with people who have significant influence.

Resonate, Don't Just Connect:
Fostering Creative, Community-Driven Relationships in Louisville and Kentucky

- **Local Business Organizations**: Joining groups like the Kentucky Chamber of Commerce, local networking groups, or sector-specific associations can help you connect with important players in the business community.

- **Social Media and Digital Platforms**: Platforms like LinkedIn can help you identify key influencers in your industry and make connections online before meeting in person.

Once you've identified key influencers, take the time to engage with them thoughtfully. Rather than immediately seeking something from them, focus on building a relationship based on mutual respect and shared interests.

Cultivate Relationships Through Reciprocity

One of the most important principles of leveraging your network is reciprocity. In Kentucky, where trust and community are core values, relationships are often built on a foundation of giving and receiving. Before asking for favors, consider how you can offer value to the other person.

Reciprocity can take many forms, including:

- **Sharing Knowledge**: If you have expertise in an area that could benefit someone in your network, offer to share that knowledge. This could be

Resonate, Don't Just Connect:
Fostering Creative, Community-Driven Relationships in Louisville and Kentucky

through consulting, providing advice, or offering resources.

- **Making Introductions**: Introduce people in your network to one another if you believe they could benefit from the connection. This not only helps others but also positions you as a connector within your community.

- **Offering Support**: If someone in your network is launching a new project, hosting an event, or facing a business challenge, offer your support. This could mean attending their event, sharing their work with your network, or providing assistance in overcoming a challenge.

In Kentucky's close-knit business community, offering value without expecting immediate returns helps build trust and fosters long-term relationships. When the time comes to leverage these relationships for business growth, people will be more inclined to support you because they know you've invested in the relationship.

Nurturing Relationships Over Time

Building high-value connections is just the beginning; nurturing those relationships over time is what allows you to leverage them for business growth. In Kentucky, where relationships are often long-term and deeply rooted, it's

Resonate, Don't Just Connect:
Fostering Creative, Community-Driven Relationships in Louisville and Kentucky

important to stay in touch and continue offering value even when you don't need anything in return.

Regular check-ins, sharing updates about your business, and staying involved in your community are all ways to keep your relationships strong. Whether it's through attending local events, sending periodic emails, or engaging with your contacts on LinkedIn, maintaining consistent communication ensures that your network remains active and ready to support you when opportunities arise.

3. Converting Connections Into Business Opportunities

The ultimate goal of leveraging your network is to convert connections into business opportunities. This requires a strategic approach, clear communication, and the ability to identify when and how to engage your network for specific outcomes.

Identifying Potential Opportunities

One of the first steps in converting connections into business opportunities is identifying where those opportunities exist within your network. This might involve recognizing when someone in your network has a need that aligns with your business offering or when a connection can introduce you to a potential partner or client.

Resonate, Don't Just Connect:
Fostering Creative, Community-Driven Relationships in Louisville and Kentucky

Consider the following scenarios for identifying opportunities:

- **Collaborations and Partnerships**: If you run a tech startup in Louisville, you might identify an opportunity to collaborate with a healthcare company in Lexington to develop new solutions for telemedicine. By leveraging your network in both cities, you can propose a partnership that benefits both parties.

- **Client Acquisition**: If you're in the bourbon industry, your network might include restaurant owners, distributors, or retailers who are potential clients. By maintaining strong relationships with these connections, you can reach out when the time is right to pitch your product or service.

- **Investment Opportunities**: If you're seeking investment for your business, look to your network for individuals or organizations that might be interested in funding your venture. Kentucky has a growing startup ecosystem, and there are many local investors and venture capitalists who are open to supporting new businesses, particularly in sectors like healthcare, technology, and bourbon.

Once you've identified a potential opportunity, it's important to approach it with clear communication and a

Resonate, Don't Just Connect:
Fostering Creative, Community-Driven Relationships in Louisville and Kentucky

well-thought-out plan for how the relationship can be mutually beneficial.

Communicating Your Value Proposition

When reaching out to your network to convert a connection into an opportunity, it's essential to communicate your value proposition clearly. Whether you're proposing a partnership, pitching a new client, or seeking investment, the other party needs to understand how working with you will benefit them.

For example, if you're proposing a partnership to a Kentucky-based logistics company, you might frame your value proposition around how your expertise in supply chain optimization can help them reduce costs and improve efficiency. Be specific about the benefits and how your collaboration will create value for both parties.

In Kentucky's business culture, where trust and mutual respect are critical, it's also important to frame the opportunity as a win-win situation. Show that you're not just looking to take advantage of the relationship but are genuinely interested in creating value for both sides.

Following Through with Action

Once you've secured an opportunity through your network, the next step is to follow through with action. This is where many professionals fall short—failing to

Resonate, Don't Just Connect:
Fostering Creative, Community-Driven Relationships in Louisville and Kentucky

deliver on promises can damage relationships and limit future opportunities.

In Kentucky, where reputation is key, following through with action is essential for maintaining trust. If you've committed to a partnership, client relationship, or collaboration, ensure that you deliver on your promises and exceed expectations whenever possible. This not only solidifies the current opportunity but also strengthens your reputation within your network, leading to future opportunities.

4. Scaling Business Growth Through Your Network

As your network grows and you begin leveraging it for business opportunities, you'll find that the possibilities for scaling your business expand as well. In Kentucky, where industries like manufacturing, healthcare, and bourbon are experiencing rapid growth, leveraging your network can help you scale your business more quickly and efficiently.

Expanding into New Markets

One of the most effective ways to scale your business is by leveraging your network to expand into new markets. For example, if your business is based in Louisville but you want to expand into Lexington or Northern Kentucky, your existing connections can provide introductions to key players in those regions. By tapping into their local

Resonate, Don't Just Connect:
Fostering Creative, Community-Driven Relationships in Louisville and Kentucky

knowledge and relationships, you can enter new markets with greater ease and less risk.

Similarly, if you're looking to expand beyond Kentucky, your network can help you make connections in other states or even internationally. For instance, Kentucky's bourbon industry has a strong global presence, and leveraging international connections can help distillers expand their market reach.

Accessing Resources and Capital

Scaling a business often requires access to additional resources, whether that's capital, talent, or technology. Your network can be a valuable resource for securing these assets. For example, if you're looking for investors to fund your growth, your network can connect you with potential investors who are interested in your industry.

In Kentucky's entrepreneurial ecosystem, there are numerous organizations, such as the Kentucky Innovation Network and local venture capital firms, that focus on supporting business growth. By leveraging your network to access these resources, you can accelerate your growth and take your business to the next level.

Innovating and Staying Competitive

As your business grows, it's important to stay competitive and continue innovating. Your network can be a valuable source of new ideas, technologies, and best practices that

Resonate, Don't Just Connect:
Fostering Creative, Community-Driven Relationships in Louisville and Kentucky

can help you stay ahead of the curve. Whether it's collaborating with industry peers to solve common challenges or learning from thought leaders in your field, your network provides access to the knowledge and insights needed to drive innovation.

In Kentucky's healthcare or tech sectors, for example, staying competitive means keeping up with rapidly evolving technologies and regulatory changes. By leveraging your network to stay informed and connected with industry trends, you can ensure that your business remains agile and competitive in a fast-changing environment.

5. Maintaining and Growing Your Network Over Time

As you continue to leverage your network for business growth, it's important to keep expanding and nurturing those relationships over time. In Kentucky, where personal connections and community involvement are central to business success, maintaining and growing your network is an ongoing process.

Attending Events and Engaging with Your Community

Staying engaged in your local business community is one of the most effective ways to grow your network. Attending industry events, joining local business

Resonate, Don't Just Connect:
Fostering Creative, Community-Driven Relationships in Louisville and Kentucky

organizations, and participating in community initiatives not only keep you connected but also help you build new relationships.

In Kentucky, there are numerous opportunities to engage with the local business community, from the annual Kentucky Bourbon Festival to healthcare summits, manufacturing expos, and local chamber of commerce events. By staying active in these events, you can continue expanding your network and uncover new opportunities for business growth.

Staying Connected Digitally

In addition to attending local events, maintaining your network digitally through platforms like LinkedIn is essential. Regularly engaging with your connections online, sharing updates about your business, and offering value through articles or insights helps keep your network engaged and ready to support you.

Investing in Long-Term Relationships

Finally, remember that leveraging your network for business growth is not a one-time effort. It requires ongoing investment in long-term relationships. By continuing to offer value, staying engaged, and nurturing your connections, you can build a network that supports your business growth for years to come.

Resonate, Don't Just Connect:
Fostering Creative, Community-Driven Relationships in Louisville and Kentucky

Conclusion: Turning Connections Into Growth in Kentucky

Leveraging your network for business growth is both an art and a science. In Kentucky, where community, trust, and relationships are the foundation of business success, the ability to turn connections into opportunities is a critical skill. By building high-value connections, offering value through reciprocity, and strategically converting relationships into opportunities, you can unlock the full potential of your network and drive significant business growth.

As Kentucky's industries continue to evolve and expand, those who master the art of leveraging their networks will be well-positioned to thrive in this dynamic business environment. Whether you're in bourbon, healthcare, manufacturing, or any other industry, your network is one of your most valuable assets—use it wisely, and the opportunities for growth will follow.

Resonate, Don't Just Connect:
Fostering Creative, Community-Driven Relationships in Louisville and Kentucky

Chapter 7: Creating a Win-Win Culture – Building Long-Term Partnerships that Benefit All Parties

In Kentucky, where community ties run deep, relationships are often forged on the principles of mutual benefit, trust, and collaboration. Whether in Louisville's burgeoning tech scene, the state's iconic bourbon industry, or the agricultural heartland, creating a "win-win" culture is not only a strategy for growth but a way of doing business that resonates with Kentucky's values. A win-win culture focuses on building long-term partnerships where both parties gain value, ensuring that the relationship is sustainable, mutually rewarding, and resilient.

This chapter will explore how to build long-term partnerships that benefit all parties, particularly within the context of Kentucky's unique industries and business landscape. We'll delve into the principles of collaboration, transparency, and shared goals that are essential for fostering a win-win culture. Additionally, we'll discuss actionable strategies for creating partnerships that are rooted in trust, mutual respect, and long-term success.

Resonate, Don't Just Connect:
Fostering Creative, Community-Driven Relationships in Louisville and Kentucky

1. Understanding the Win-Win Mindset

Before diving into the tactics of building partnerships, it's important to understand what a win-win culture truly means. At its core, a win-win partnership is one in which all parties involved benefit in some meaningful way. Unlike transactional relationships, where one party often benefits at the expense of the other, win-win relationships are collaborative, with a focus on creating value for everyone involved.

The Kentucky Context: Why Win-Win Matters

Kentucky's business environment is built on relationships, community involvement, and shared success. From the bourbon distilleries of Bardstown to the healthcare hubs of Lexington and Louisville, businesses in Kentucky often operate in a way that reflects the state's cultural values—emphasizing collaboration, trust, and fairness. In such an environment, building a win-win culture is not just a best practice; it's essential for long-term success.

In industries like bourbon, for example, distilleries work closely with local farmers, suppliers, and distributors. These relationships are typically long-term, and both parties depend on one another for success. If one party suffers—whether due to pricing issues, supply chain disruptions, or market downturns—the other party often feels the effects as well. Therefore, building partnerships

Resonate, Don't Just Connect:
Fostering Creative, Community-Driven Relationships in Louisville and Kentucky

where both sides are invested in each other's success is key to creating stability and fostering growth.

In Kentucky's healthcare sector, hospitals and healthcare providers often collaborate with tech companies, pharmaceutical suppliers, and research institutions. These partnerships succeed when both parties work toward shared goals—such as improving patient care, reducing costs, or advancing medical research—while ensuring that both sides derive tangible value from the collaboration.

A win-win culture thrives when businesses see their partners as allies rather than competitors or mere service providers. By shifting the focus to long-term success for all parties, businesses can build resilient partnerships that weather challenges and create sustainable growth.

2. The Foundations of a Win-Win Culture

Creating a win-win culture starts with establishing a strong foundation built on shared values, clear communication, and mutual respect. In Kentucky, where relationships are often formed through trust and personal connections, laying the groundwork for a win-win partnership is essential for building long-term success.

Shared Values and Alignment

One of the most critical components of a win-win partnership is having shared values and goals. Whether you're entering into a business deal, forming a strategic

Resonate, Don't Just Connect:
Fostering Creative, Community-Driven Relationships in Louisville and Kentucky

alliance, or collaborating on a project, alignment between partners is key to ensuring long-term success.

In Kentucky's business environment, shared values often revolve around community involvement, ethical practices, and a commitment to mutual benefit. For example, many Kentucky-based companies prioritize supporting local suppliers, reinvesting in the community, and promoting sustainability. By aligning on these values, businesses can create partnerships that resonate with both their internal stakeholders and the broader community.

When approaching potential partnerships, it's important to ask the following questions:

- **Do we share similar goals and values?** Understanding what drives both parties is essential for building trust and ensuring that the partnership is built on a foundation of mutual respect and shared purpose.

- **How do our long-term visions align?** A win-win partnership requires that both parties are working toward a future where everyone benefits. It's important to ensure that your vision for the partnership aligns with your partner's goals and that both sides see the long-term value in the relationship.

Resonate, Don't Just Connect:
Fostering Creative, Community-Driven Relationships in Louisville and Kentucky

In Kentucky's agriculture sector, for example, farmers and food producers often collaborate on sustainability initiatives, ensuring that their operations benefit both the environment and the local community. By aligning on shared values—such as reducing waste, improving land stewardship, or promoting locally sourced products—these partnerships create a win-win scenario where both the farmers and producers benefit, along with the broader community.

Open and Transparent Communication

Clear communication is at the heart of any successful win-win partnership. Without open, honest communication, misunderstandings and misaligned expectations can derail even the most promising partnerships. In Kentucky, where relationships are often built on trust and personal connections, transparency is especially important.

Open communication involves more than just regular check-ins; it's about being upfront about expectations, challenges, and opportunities. For a partnership to truly benefit both parties, each side must feel comfortable sharing information, addressing concerns, and discussing how to maximize the value of the collaboration.

Some key principles of open communication in a win-win culture include:

Resonate, Don't Just Connect:
Fostering Creative, Community-Driven Relationships in Louisville and Kentucky

- **Setting clear expectations from the beginning**: Before entering into any partnership, both parties should clearly articulate their goals, responsibilities, and expectations. This ensures that everyone is on the same page and minimizes the risk of misunderstandings.

- **Regularly reviewing progress and goals**: Once the partnership is underway, both parties should take the time to regularly review progress, assess performance, and discuss any changes in goals or strategies. This creates a sense of accountability and ensures that the partnership remains aligned over time.

- **Addressing challenges openly**: No partnership is without challenges. The key to overcoming obstacles in a win-win culture is addressing them openly and collaboratively. When challenges arise, both parties should work together to find solutions that benefit everyone involved, rather than trying to place blame or prioritize their own interests.

In Kentucky's logistics industry, companies often work closely with partners across the supply chain, from manufacturers to transportation providers. Open and transparent communication between these partners is essential for ensuring that goods are delivered on time and

Resonate, Don't Just Connect:
Fostering Creative, Community-Driven Relationships in Louisville and Kentucky

that both sides can adjust to changing conditions, such as delays or supply chain disruptions. By maintaining open lines of communication, businesses in this sector can create a win-win culture where both sides work together to solve problems and achieve shared success.

Mutual Respect and Trust

Trust and respect are cornerstones of any win-win partnership. In Kentucky's business culture, where personal relationships often play a large role in decision-making, trust is especially important. A successful win-win culture cannot exist without mutual respect between partners.

Trust is built over time through consistent behavior, open communication, and a commitment to the success of the partnership. When both parties trust one another, they are more likely to collaborate openly, share resources, and invest in the long-term health of the relationship.

Respect in a partnership means recognizing the value that each party brings to the table. In a win-win culture, both sides should feel that their contributions are appreciated and that their input is taken seriously. This mutual respect fosters a collaborative environment where both parties are invested in each other's success.

For example, in Kentucky's bourbon industry, many distilleries have long-standing relationships with local farmers who provide the grains used in bourbon production. These partnerships are built on trust and mutual respect, as both sides recognize the importance of each other's contributions. The distillery relies on the farmer for high-quality ingredients, while the farmer relies on the distillery for consistent business. By fostering a win-win culture based on respect and trust, both parties can succeed in the long run.

3. Strategies for Building Long-Term Win-Win Partnerships

Building a win-win culture doesn't happen overnight. It requires intentional effort, strategic thinking, and a commitment to creating value for all parties involved. The following strategies can help you build long-term partnerships that benefit everyone, whether you're in Kentucky's healthcare sector, manufacturing industry, or any other field.

1. Focus on Creating Mutual Value

At the heart of a win-win culture is the idea of creating mutual value. Both parties should feel that they are gaining something meaningful from the partnership. This doesn't necessarily mean that both sides have to receive the same type of benefit, but there should be a sense of balance in the value exchange.

Resonate, Don't Just Connect:
Fostering Creative, Community-Driven Relationships in Louisville and Kentucky

For example, in Kentucky's healthcare industry, a hospital may partner with a tech company to develop new patient care technologies. While the hospital benefits from improved patient outcomes, the tech company gains valuable insights into healthcare needs and may develop products that it can market to other hospitals. Both parties benefit, but in different ways. The key is ensuring that both sides perceive the partnership as valuable and worthwhile.

When negotiating partnerships, it's important to:

- **Understand each other's needs and goals**: Take the time to understand what your partner needs from the relationship and how your business can help meet those needs. Likewise, communicate your own goals clearly to ensure that the partnership aligns with your business objectives.

- **Look for win-win solutions**: When challenges arise, work together to find solutions that benefit both parties. Rather than focusing on who is right or wrong, focus on how you can create value for everyone involved.

- **Be flexible and open to compromise**: A win-win culture requires flexibility and a willingness to compromise. Both parties should be open to adjusting their approach to ensure that the partnership remains mutually beneficial.

Resonate, Don't Just Connect:
Fostering Creative, Community-Driven Relationships in Louisville and Kentucky

2. Invest in Long-Term Success

A key component of a win-win culture is a focus on long-term success rather than short-term gains. While short-term wins can be valuable, the true strength of a win-win partnership comes from the ability to create sustainable growth over time.

In Kentucky's business environment, many successful partnerships have stood the test of time because both parties invested in each other's long-term success. Whether it's a distributor and manufacturer working together to navigate supply chain challenges or a healthcare provider and tech company collaborating on a multi-year project, long-term investments in the partnership lead to better outcomes.

To build long-term partnerships, consider the following:

- **Set long-term goals**: When entering into a partnership, set clear long-term goals that benefit both parties. These goals should focus on sustainability, growth, and the overall health of the partnership.

- **Reinvest in the partnership**: As the partnership progresses, look for opportunities to reinvest in the relationship. This could mean expanding the scope of the collaboration, exploring new areas of

Resonate, Don't Just Connect:
Fostering Creative, Community-Driven Relationships in Louisville and Kentucky

business, or providing additional resources to help your partner succeed.

- **Be patient and committed**: Building a long-term win-win partnership requires patience and commitment. Challenges will inevitably arise, but staying focused on the long-term benefits can help both parties navigate difficulties and emerge stronger.

For example, Kentucky's horse racing industry relies on long-term partnerships between breeders, trainers, and jockeys. These partnerships are built on mutual trust, and both sides invest in each other's success to ensure that they remain competitive in the long run.

3. Collaborate on Innovation and Problem-Solving

One of the most exciting aspects of a win-win culture is the potential for innovation and problem-solving. When both parties are invested in each other's success, they are more likely to collaborate on new ideas, technologies, and solutions that benefit everyone.

In Kentucky's manufacturing sector, companies often collaborate with suppliers and tech firms to develop innovative solutions that improve efficiency, reduce costs, or address industry challenges. By working together to solve problems, both sides can create new opportunities for growth and success.

Resonate, Don't Just Connect:
Fostering Creative, Community-Driven Relationships in Louisville and Kentucky

To foster a culture of collaboration and innovation:

- **Encourage open dialogue**: Create a partnership environment where both parties feel comfortable sharing ideas and brainstorming solutions. Innovation thrives in open, collaborative spaces.

- **Be open to new ideas**: A win-win culture requires a willingness to try new approaches and explore new possibilities. Be open to experimenting with different strategies or technologies that could benefit both sides.

- **Celebrate shared successes**: When a partnership leads to a successful innovation or solution, take the time to celebrate that success together. Recognizing and celebrating shared wins reinforces the value of the partnership and encourages future collaboration.

4. Build Partnerships Beyond Business Transactions

A true win-win culture goes beyond simple business transactions. It's about building relationships that extend beyond the immediate deal or project. In Kentucky, where personal relationships and community involvement play a large role in business success, building deeper connections with your partners can create long-lasting, mutually beneficial relationships.

To build partnerships beyond business transactions:

Resonate, Don't Just Connect:
Fostering Creative, Community-Driven Relationships in Louisville and Kentucky

- **Engage with your partner's community**: Whether it's supporting local initiatives, attending community events, or participating in industry groups, engaging with your partner's community shows that you are invested in their success beyond the business deal.

- **Foster personal relationships**: Take the time to get to know your partners on a personal level. Building strong personal relationships helps create trust and makes the partnership more resilient.

- **Look for opportunities to give back**: A win-win culture is about creating value for everyone involved, including the broader community. Look for ways to give back to the community or support causes that both you and your partner care about.

In Kentucky's bourbon industry, many distilleries have built long-term partnerships with local farmers, suppliers, and distributors by supporting community initiatives, engaging with industry groups, and fostering personal relationships. These partnerships extend beyond business transactions and contribute to the overall success of the local economy.

4. Case Studies of Win-Win Partnerships in Kentucky

Resonate, Don't Just Connect:
Fostering Creative, Community-Driven Relationships in Louisville and Kentucky

To illustrate how a win-win culture can be implemented in practice, let's explore a few examples of successful partnerships in Kentucky.

Case Study 1: The Bourbon Industry and Local Farmers

Kentucky's bourbon industry is known for its long-standing partnerships with local farmers who supply the grains used in bourbon production. These partnerships are built on mutual trust, shared goals, and a commitment to sustainability. By working together, distilleries and farmers create a win-win scenario where both sides benefit: the distilleries receive high-quality grains, and the farmers receive consistent business and support for sustainable farming practices.

This win-win culture has helped the bourbon industry thrive while also contributing to the success of local agriculture. Both parties are invested in each other's long-term success, and the partnership creates value not only for the businesses involved but also for the broader community.

Case Study 2: Healthcare and Technology Collaboration

In Lexington, a local hospital partnered with a tech startup to develop new telemedicine solutions for rural areas of Kentucky. The partnership was designed as a win-win scenario: the hospital improved patient access to care, while the tech startup gained valuable insights and a new market for its products.

The collaboration led to the development of a successful telemedicine platform that benefited both parties and, more importantly, provided much-needed healthcare services to rural communities. The partnership has since expanded, with both sides continuing to innovate and collaborate on new healthcare solutions.

Case Study 3: Logistics and Manufacturing Partnership

In Northern Kentucky, a logistics company partnered with a manufacturing firm to streamline the supply chain for automotive parts. The partnership was based on a win-win approach, with both companies working together to reduce costs, improve delivery times, and enhance overall efficiency.

By sharing resources, expertise, and technology, both companies benefited from the collaboration, leading to increased profitability and customer satisfaction. The partnership has become a model for other businesses in Kentucky's logistics and manufacturing sectors, demonstrating the power of a win-win culture.

Conclusion: Building a Win-Win Culture in Kentucky

Resonate, Don't Just Connect:
Fostering Creative, Community-Driven Relationships in Louisville and Kentucky

Creating a win-win culture is essential for building long-term partnerships that benefit all parties involved. In Kentucky's unique business landscape, where relationships, trust, and community values are paramount, fostering a win-win mindset can lead to sustainable growth, innovation, and shared success.

By focusing on mutual value, open communication, and long-term investments in each other's success, businesses in Kentucky can build partnerships that are resilient, rewarding, and built to last. Whether you're in bourbon, healthcare, manufacturing, or any other industry, a win-win culture is the key to unlocking new opportunities and driving business growth in the Bluegrass State.

Resonate, Don't Just Connect:
Fostering Creative, Community-Driven Relationships in Louisville and Kentucky

Chapter 8: Overcoming Networking Anxiety – How to Approach Networking When You're an Introvert or Uncomfortable

Networking is often regarded as an essential skill for professional success, but for many individuals, particularly introverts or those who feel uncomfortable in social situations, networking can provoke significant anxiety. The thought of attending large events, striking up conversations with strangers, and presenting yourself in front of influential people can be overwhelming. However, networking does not have to be intimidating, even for introverts. In fact, some of the most effective networkers are individuals who have learned how to navigate these environments in a way that feels authentic and comfortable to them.

In Kentucky, a state that values community, relationships, and mutual support, networking is especially crucial. Whether you're working in Louisville's bustling business sector, Lexington's healthcare and education fields, or in more rural areas connected to agriculture or manufacturing, building and maintaining relationships is key to success. Fortunately, there are strategies that can

Resonate, Don't Just Connect:
Fostering Creative, Community-Driven Relationships in Louisville and Kentucky

help even the most introverted professionals overcome their networking anxiety and thrive in Kentucky's relationship-driven business culture.

This chapter will explore how introverts and those who feel uncomfortable with traditional networking can successfully approach networking opportunities in Kentucky. We will look at practical strategies to manage anxiety, ways to build confidence, and how to form meaningful connections that are authentic to who you are, without forcing you into an extroverted mold.

1. Understanding Networking Anxiety

Networking anxiety often stems from a fear of judgment, rejection, or failure in social situations. For introverts, this anxiety can be compounded by the natural tendency to feel drained by social interactions, particularly in large groups. The idea of having to "perform" in front of others, whether at a business event or a casual gathering, can feel overwhelming.

The Kentucky Business Culture

Kentucky's business environment, while relationship-oriented, also places high value on authenticity and trust. While networking may seem daunting, it's important to understand that successful networking in Kentucky is not about putting on a show or being the loudest person in the room. It's about making genuine, lasting connections that

Resonate, Don't Just Connect:
Fostering Creative, Community-Driven Relationships in Louisville and Kentucky

benefit both parties. This means that introverts and those who are uncomfortable with traditional networking actually have an advantage—they tend to be great listeners, thoughtful in their interactions, and more likely to build deep, meaningful relationships over time.

By reframing your approach to networking, you can shift your focus from "performing" to building real, valuable connections. In Kentucky, where communities are often small and interconnected, authenticity is more important than ever, and networking can be about quality over quantity.

2. Preparing for Networking Opportunities

One of the most effective ways to overcome networking anxiety is through preparation. Just as an athlete prepares before a big game, you can approach networking events with a strategy that helps you feel more in control and confident. This preparation is particularly helpful for introverts, who may need more time to feel comfortable entering a new environment.

Research the Event and Attendees

Knowing who will be attending an event and what topics will be discussed can help alleviate the anxiety of the unknown. In Kentucky, where many industries like bourbon, agriculture, healthcare, and logistics are tightly interconnected, it's likely that you'll encounter people

Resonate, Don't Just Connect:
Fostering Creative, Community-Driven Relationships in Louisville and Kentucky

who are already familiar with your work or industry. Taking time to research attendees and identifying potential people you'd like to meet helps you approach the event with a sense of purpose, rather than feeling like you're walking in blind.

Start by considering:

- **Who is attending?** Look at the attendee list or review the event's speakers, exhibitors, or sponsors. This gives you a clearer picture of who you might meet and allows you to identify specific individuals you'd like to connect with.

- **What's the agenda?** If the event has a published schedule, review it in advance to identify the sessions or activities that are most relevant to you. Knowing the flow of the event helps reduce anxiety by providing structure to your experience.

- **What are your goals?** Clarifying what you hope to achieve—whether it's learning about a new industry trend, meeting a potential collaborator, or simply expanding your network—will help focus your efforts and reduce anxiety.

For example, if you're attending a healthcare conference in Lexington, you might focus on connecting with local professionals who specialize in telemedicine, a rapidly growing field in Kentucky's healthcare industry.

Resonate, Don't Just Connect:
Fostering Creative, Community-Driven Relationships in Louisville and Kentucky

Knowing that you'll be interacting with people who share your interests or professional goals can help you feel more comfortable and confident.

Prepare an Elevator Pitch

Having a prepared elevator pitch—an introduction that succinctly explains who you are, what you do, and why you're there—can provide a sense of security in networking situations. A good elevator pitch is brief (about 30 seconds) and highlights your value without overwhelming the listener.

For introverts or those with networking anxiety, practicing your elevator pitch can help you feel more comfortable entering conversations. It gives you a starting point and ensures that you're ready when someone asks, "What do you do?"

For example, if you work in Kentucky's logistics industry, your elevator pitch might sound like this:

"Hi, I'm [Your Name]. I work in supply chain management, specializing in optimizing distribution networks across Kentucky. With our state being a major logistics hub, I'm passionate about helping companies streamline their operations and improve efficiency. I'm here to learn about the latest trends in supply chain technology and connect with others who are working in this field."

Resonate, Don't Just Connect:
Fostering Creative, Community-Driven Relationships in Louisville and Kentucky

By practicing this ahead of time, you'll feel more confident when you're introduced to new people.

Set Realistic Expectations

One of the reasons networking can feel overwhelming is because people often feel pressure to meet as many people as possible or make a lasting impression on everyone they meet. However, quality is more important than quantity, especially for introverts. Rather than trying to network with dozens of people, set a goal to have meaningful conversations with just a few individuals.

For example, if you're attending a business expo in Louisville, you might set a goal to connect with three or four people who share your professional interests. This takes the pressure off and makes the event feel more manageable.

3. Managing Anxiety During the Event

Even with preparation, attending a networking event can still cause anxiety, particularly for introverts or those uncomfortable in social settings. However, there are several techniques you can use to manage your anxiety and make the experience more enjoyable.

Start with Small Groups or One-on-One Conversations

Resonate, Don't Just Connect:
Fostering Creative, Community-Driven Relationships in Louisville and Kentucky

Large groups can be intimidating, especially for introverts. If the idea of mingling in a crowd feels overwhelming, look for opportunities to start with smaller groups or one-on-one conversations. In Kentucky's business culture, which values personal connections, you'll often find that people are open to quieter, more intimate conversations.

For example, if you're attending a conference, you might begin by approaching someone who is standing alone or joining a small group rather than jumping into a large crowd. Starting small can help you build confidence and ease into the event.

Use Active Listening to Your Advantage

Introverts are often naturally good listeners, and this is a valuable asset in networking situations. Rather than feeling pressure to talk or "perform," focus on being an active listener. Ask thoughtful questions and show genuine interest in what the other person is saying. This takes the pressure off you to constantly speak and allows you to engage in meaningful conversations.

In Kentucky's relationship-driven business environment, people appreciate when someone takes the time to listen and engage in thoughtful dialogue. By being a good listener, you can build strong connections without feeling like you need to dominate the conversation.

Resonate, Don't Just Connect:
Fostering Creative, Community-Driven Relationships in Louisville and Kentucky

For example, if you're speaking with someone in Kentucky's bourbon industry, you might ask, "What inspired you to get involved in this industry?" or "How do you see the future of bourbon production evolving in Kentucky?" These types of questions not only show genuine interest but also help keep the conversation flowing naturally.

Take Breaks When Needed

It's important to recognize that networking can be draining, especially for introverts. Don't be afraid to take breaks when you need them. Stepping away from the crowd for a few minutes—whether to grab a drink, check your phone, or take a walk—can help you recharge and reduce feelings of overwhelm.

Kentucky's business events often offer natural breaks, such as networking receptions, lunch breaks, or coffee breaks, which provide opportunities to regroup and reset before diving back into the event.

4. Building Confidence Through Practice

Like any skill, networking becomes easier with practice. The more you expose yourself to networking situations, the more comfortable and confident you'll become over time. While it may never feel entirely natural for introverts or those with social anxiety, each experience helps build confidence and resilience.

Resonate, Don't Just Connect:
Fostering Creative, Community-Driven Relationships in Louisville and Kentucky

Start with Low-Stakes Networking

If large conferences or high-pressure business events feel overwhelming, start with lower-stakes networking opportunities. These might include smaller industry meetups, local chamber of commerce events, or even virtual networking sessions. Kentucky has a vibrant small business community, and there are plenty of opportunities to network in more relaxed, informal settings.

For example, if you're based in Louisville and work in the tech industry, you might attend a local tech meetup rather than a large national conference. These smaller events offer the chance to practice networking in a more intimate environment, helping you build confidence before tackling larger events.

Focus on Building Relationships Over Time

One of the reasons networking can feel daunting is the expectation to form immediate, deep connections. However, networking is about building relationships over time, not forcing instant connections. Instead of focusing on what you can get from each interaction, approach networking with the mindset of building relationships gradually.

In Kentucky's business culture, relationships often develop over time through repeated interactions. You might meet someone at a conference, follow up with them

Resonate, Don't Just Connect:
Fostering Creative, Community-Driven Relationships in Louisville and Kentucky

afterward, and then connect again at a future event. By focusing on the long game, you can take the pressure off each individual interaction and allow relationships to develop naturally.

For example, if you meet someone in Kentucky's agriculture industry at a local event, you can follow up with a friendly email afterward and suggest connecting over coffee in the future. This takes the pressure off the initial meeting and allows the relationship to grow at a comfortable pace.

Practice Networking Outside of Traditional Settings

Networking doesn't always have to take place at formal events. In fact, some of the best networking happens in more casual, everyday settings. Kentucky is known for its community-oriented culture, and you may find networking opportunities at local gatherings, community events, or even social settings.

For instance, attending local events like the Kentucky Bourbon Festival or charity fundraisers in Lexington can provide a more relaxed environment to connect with others who share your interests. These informal settings often feel less intimidating and offer opportunities to practice your networking skills in a more comfortable context.

Resonate, Don't Just Connect:
Fostering Creative, Community-Driven Relationships in Louisville and Kentucky

5. Networking for Introverts in Kentucky's Key Industries

Kentucky's unique business landscape provides ample opportunities for introverts to network effectively, particularly in industries where personal relationships are key. By focusing on authentic connections and taking advantage of Kentucky's relationship-driven culture, introverts can thrive in their networking efforts.

Bourbon Industry

In Kentucky's bourbon industry, personal connections and long-term relationships are crucial to success. Whether you're attending a distillery event, a bourbon festival, or a trade show, networking in this industry often revolves around building trust and maintaining relationships over time.

For introverts, this industry's focus on authenticity and craftsmanship provides an opportunity to connect with others who share a passion for the craft. You don't need to be the loudest person in the room to make an impact; simply being genuine and showing interest in others' work can help you build meaningful connections.

Healthcare and Education

Kentucky is home to a thriving healthcare and education sector, particularly in cities like Lexington and Louisville. Networking in these industries often takes place in conferences, panel discussions, and academic forums. For introverts, the key is to focus on thought leadership and knowledge sharing.

If you're attending a healthcare or education event, position yourself as a listener and learner. Ask insightful questions during discussions, and engage in one-on-one conversations with speakers or attendees. In these knowledge-driven industries, showing that you're thoughtful and informed can help you build connections without needing to be extroverted.

Agriculture and Manufacturing

In Kentucky's agriculture and manufacturing sectors, many networking opportunities arise through local trade shows, business expos, and industry associations. These industries often value hands-on experience and practical knowledge, which can be a strong advantage for introverts who prefer in-depth, meaningful conversations.

At agriculture expos or manufacturing events, focus on connecting with others by discussing shared challenges and exchanging insights about industry trends. Introverts often excel in these more technical or specialized conversations, where depth of knowledge matters more than small talk.

6. Follow-Up Strategies for Introverts

Resonate, Don't Just Connect:
Fostering Creative, Community-Driven Relationships in Louisville and Kentucky

One of the most important aspects of networking is the follow-up. For introverts, the follow-up process can feel less intimidating than in-person interactions, as it provides an opportunity to build relationships in a more controlled and comfortable environment.

Personalized Follow-Ups

When following up after an event, be sure to personalize your messages. Reference your conversation with the person and express genuine interest in staying connected. Kentucky's business culture values authenticity, so taking the time to craft a thoughtful message goes a long way.

For example:

"Hi [Name],
It was great meeting you at the [Event Name] in Louisville. I really enjoyed our conversation about [topic discussed], and I'd love to stay connected. Let me know if you'd be interested in grabbing coffee sometime to continue the discussion!
Best,
[Your Name]"

Use LinkedIn for Ongoing Engagement

LinkedIn is a valuable tool for introverts, as it allows you to engage with your network in a low-pressure, online environment. After an event, connect with the people you met on LinkedIn, and engage with their posts by liking, commenting, or sharing. This keeps you on their radar without the need for constant in-person interactions.

Offer Value in Your Follow-Ups

Instead of simply asking to stay in touch, look for ways to offer value to the person you're following up with. This could be sharing an article relevant to their interests, introducing them to someone in your network, or offering a resource that might benefit them. By focusing on giving rather than taking, you can build strong, mutually beneficial relationships.

Conclusion: Networking with Confidence as an Introvert in Kentucky

Networking doesn't have to be a daunting experience, even for introverts or those uncomfortable in social situations. By preparing ahead of time, focusing on genuine connections, and leveraging your strengths—such as active listening and thoughtful engagement—you can approach networking with confidence and ease.

In Kentucky's business landscape, where relationships, trust, and community are central to success, networking is about building long-term, authentic connections. By focusing on quality over quantity, and by practicing your networking skills in smaller, low-pressure settings, you can overcome networking anxiety and form relationships that benefit both your career and your community.

Resonate, Don't Just Connect:
Fostering Creative, Community-Driven Relationships in Louisville and Kentucky

As you continue to develop your networking skills, remember that introverts bring unique strengths to the table, and Kentucky's collaborative, relationship-driven business culture is the perfect environment for those strengths to shine. With the right approach, you can turn networking from a source of anxiety into an opportunity for growth and success.

Resonate, Don't Just Connect:
Fostering Creative, Community-Driven Relationships in Louisville and Kentucky

Chapter 9: The Business of Giving – The Importance of Offering Value Before Asking for Favors

In the world of business, relationships are the cornerstone of success. In Kentucky, where industries such as bourbon, healthcare, manufacturing, and agriculture thrive on close-knit communities and long-standing partnerships, building genuine connections is even more important. However, successful business relationships aren't built by simply asking for favors or expecting others to offer help without reciprocity. Instead, the most effective businesspeople know the importance of offering value first—before seeking anything in return.

The philosophy of "give before you get" isn't just a strategy; it's a mindset. When you prioritize giving, you're focusing on creating mutual value, building trust, and fostering long-term relationships that can ultimately benefit everyone involved. This principle resonates strongly with Kentucky's culture of hospitality, trust, and community. Whether you're based in Louisville's thriving business sector or working in more rural areas connected to agriculture or bourbon production, offering value first

Resonate, Don't Just Connect:
Fostering Creative, Community-Driven Relationships in Louisville and Kentucky

is key to unlocking opportunities and cultivating relationships that last.

This chapter explores how the business of giving works in Kentucky's unique environment. We'll discuss why offering value is crucial, how it builds trust and long-term relationships, and actionable ways to provide value in various business situations. Ultimately, the goal is to understand that by giving without expectation, you create a foundation for success that not only benefits you but also strengthens the entire community.

1. Why Offering Value First Matters

The idea of offering value before asking for favors goes beyond simple business etiquette—it's about demonstrating that you are invested in the success of others, which in turn helps build relationships based on trust and mutual respect. When you focus on giving, you not only position yourself as someone who contributes to the community, but you also create an environment where people are more willing to help you when the time comes. In Kentucky, where business often operates within tight-knit communities, this approach is especially important.

Trust is the Foundation of Kentucky Business

In Kentucky, trust is a key factor in business success. Whether you're working in healthcare, manufacturing, or bourbon production, business decisions are often made

Resonate, Don't Just Connect:
Fostering Creative, Community-Driven Relationships in Louisville and Kentucky

based on relationships, personal integrity, and the reputation of those involved. In industries where word-of-mouth recommendations and personal connections carry significant weight, building trust is essential.

Offering value first is one of the most effective ways to build trust. By showing that you are willing to help others without expecting anything in return, you establish yourself as someone who is reliable, generous, and genuinely invested in the well-being of your business partners. This approach aligns with Kentucky's emphasis on community and long-term relationships.

For example, in the state's agriculture sector, relationships between farmers and suppliers are often built over decades. Offering value might involve sharing knowledge, providing resources, or supporting a partner during tough times. This reciprocal approach ensures that when you eventually need support, your partners will be there to help, based on the trust and goodwill you've built over time.

Reciprocity vs. Transactional Relationships

In a transactional relationship, each interaction is based on immediate gain. One party provides something in exchange for a specific return, and the relationship doesn't go beyond the immediate deal. While transactional relationships can be useful in some contexts, they are not conducive to long-term success, especially in

Resonate, Don't Just Connect:
Fostering Creative, Community-Driven Relationships in Louisville and Kentucky

Kentucky, where business culture values deep, enduring connections.

In contrast, relationships built on reciprocity emphasize giving without an immediate expectation of return. These relationships are more sustainable because they are based on mutual respect, trust, and a commitment to the success of both parties. Offering value first is at the core of reciprocity—it allows both parties to benefit from the relationship over time, rather than focusing solely on short-term gains.

Kentucky's bourbon industry is a perfect example of this. Many distilleries work with local farmers to source the grains used in bourbon production. The success of both parties depends on their ability to support one another, especially during challenging seasons or economic fluctuations. By offering value—whether through fair pricing, reliable supply chains, or collaborative problem-solving—distilleries and farmers create long-lasting relationships that benefit both sides.

The Long Game: Building Relationships for the Future

In Kentucky, where industries are often deeply interconnected, business is rarely a one-time interaction. Success comes from cultivating relationships that stand the test of time. When you offer value first, you are playing the long game—investing in relationships that

Resonate, Don't Just Connect:
Fostering Creative, Community-Driven Relationships in Louisville and Kentucky

may not yield immediate results but will pay dividends in the future.

For instance, if you're a healthcare professional in Lexington and you offer to mentor a younger colleague or share resources with a local clinic, you're not doing it for immediate gain. Instead, you're building relationships that could lead to future collaborations, partnerships, or referrals. By focusing on the long-term benefits, you ensure that your network continues to grow and strengthen over time.

2. Ways to Offer Value in Business

Offering value in business doesn't always mean giving away products or services for free. There are many ways to provide value that can build strong relationships, enhance your reputation, and position you as a trusted partner. In Kentucky's business environment, where community and collaboration are highly valued, there are several strategies you can use to offer value in meaningful ways.

1. Share Knowledge and Expertise

One of the most valuable things you can offer in any business relationship is your knowledge and expertise. By sharing insights, offering advice, or providing access to valuable information, you demonstrate your willingness to help others succeed.

Resonate, Don't Just Connect:
Fostering Creative, Community-Driven Relationships in Louisville and Kentucky

In Kentucky's healthcare sector, for example, professionals often collaborate on research, share best practices, or mentor younger colleagues. By offering your expertise without expecting immediate compensation, you position yourself as a leader in your field and create opportunities for future partnerships.

Similarly, if you're in the tech industry in Louisville, you might offer to host a workshop or webinar to share insights on emerging technologies. This not only helps others in your community but also establishes you as a thought leader and builds goodwill within your network.

2. Make Introductions and Connections

Networking is one of the most powerful tools in business, and one of the best ways to offer value is by making introductions that benefit others. In Kentucky, where personal relationships are often the key to business success, being a connector can significantly enhance your reputation and expand your network.

For instance, if you know someone in Kentucky's logistics industry who could benefit from meeting a supplier or manufacturer you work with, making that introduction helps both parties and strengthens your relationships with them. The more you help others build their networks, the more likely they will be to reciprocate when you need support.

Resonate, Don't Just Connect:
Fostering Creative, Community-Driven Relationships in Louisville and Kentucky

Making introductions isn't about expecting a direct return; it's about creating opportunities for others to succeed, which ultimately reflects well on you as someone who fosters collaboration and growth.

3. Provide Resources or Support

Sometimes offering value means providing resources or support when someone needs it most. In Kentucky's business culture, where community support and helping others are deeply ingrained, providing resources—whether it's time, manpower, or access to your network—can have a significant impact.

For example, if you run a small business in a rural part of Kentucky and a neighboring business is struggling with a supply chain issue, offering to share resources or provide logistical support can help them navigate the challenge. This kind of assistance builds strong relationships and creates a sense of loyalty between businesses.

In larger cities like Louisville, offering value might involve providing resources for community projects, sponsoring local events, or supporting nonprofit organizations that align with your business's values. By giving back to the community, you not only enhance your reputation but also strengthen your ties to the local business ecosystem.

4. Offer Mentorship or Guidance

Resonate, Don't Just Connect:
Fostering Creative, Community-Driven Relationships in Louisville and Kentucky

Mentorship is one of the most impactful ways to offer value in business, particularly in industries that rely on personal relationships and long-term success. In Kentucky, where many industries are closely tied to local communities, offering mentorship can help cultivate the next generation of professionals while also strengthening your own network.

For example, if you're a seasoned professional in Kentucky's agriculture industry, offering to mentor a younger farmer can provide them with valuable guidance, while also building a relationship that could benefit both parties in the future. Mentorship fosters a culture of giving and learning, which ultimately benefits the entire industry.

In Kentucky's healthcare or education sectors, mentorship can involve providing guidance to new graduates, sharing career advice, or offering internships. By investing in others' success, you create a network of professionals who are likely to support you when opportunities arise.

5. Collaborate on Projects or Initiatives

Collaborating with others on projects or initiatives is another powerful way to offer value. In Kentucky's collaborative business environment, working together on shared goals helps strengthen relationships and creates opportunities for mutual success.

Resonate, Don't Just Connect:
Fostering Creative, Community-Driven Relationships in Louisville and Kentucky

For example, if you're in Kentucky's manufacturing sector, you might collaborate with a local supplier to develop more efficient production processes. This collaboration benefits both parties and strengthens the partnership for future projects.

Similarly, in the nonprofit sector, businesses in Kentucky often collaborate on community initiatives, such as sponsoring local events, supporting educational programs, or partnering on sustainability projects. These collaborations not only benefit the community but also build strong, lasting relationships between businesses and organizations.

3. The Importance of Patience and Persistence

Offering value first requires patience and persistence. Building strong business relationships takes time, and you may not see immediate returns from your efforts. However, by consistently offering value and investing in others' success, you lay the groundwork for future opportunities.

Cultivating Relationships Over Time

In Kentucky, where business relationships often develop slowly and are built on trust, it's important to cultivate relationships over time. Offering value in small, meaningful ways—whether it's through a helpful

Resonate, Don't Just Connect:
Fostering Creative, Community-Driven Relationships in Louisville and Kentucky

introduction, a shared resource, or mentorship—helps build rapport and trust.

For example, if you're in the bourbon industry and you consistently offer insights or support to your partners, those relationships will grow stronger over time. When opportunities for collaboration arise, your partners will be more likely to turn to you because they know you've invested in their success.

Handling Rejection and Setbacks

Offering value doesn't always lead to immediate success, and there will be times when your efforts aren't reciprocated right away. It's important to remember that setbacks are a natural part of building relationships, and patience is key to overcoming these challenges.

In Kentucky's agriculture industry, for example, farmers often face unpredictable challenges, from weather-related disruptions to market fluctuations. Building relationships with suppliers, buyers, and other stakeholders requires persistence, even when the immediate results aren't apparent. By continuing to offer value and support, you increase the likelihood of building strong, long-term partnerships that will benefit you in the future.

4. Kentucky Case Studies: The Business of Giving in Action

Resonate, Don't Just Connect:
Fostering Creative, Community-Driven Relationships in Louisville and Kentucky

To illustrate how the business of giving works in practice, let's explore a few case studies from Kentucky's key industries. These examples highlight how offering value first leads to long-term success and strengthens relationships across sectors.

Case Study 1: A Bourbon Distillery and Its Local Farmers

In Bardstown, known as the Bourbon Capital of the World, a local distillery has built a reputation for supporting local farmers who supply the grains for its bourbon production. Rather than focusing solely on negotiating the lowest prices, the distillery takes a collaborative approach, offering farmers fair prices, technical assistance, and long-term contracts.

By investing in the success of its suppliers, the distillery ensures a reliable, high-quality supply chain while also supporting the local agricultural community. The farmers, in turn, are more loyal to the distillery and are willing to go the extra mile to ensure the quality of the product. This win-win relationship has helped the distillery maintain consistent production, even during challenging economic times.

Case Study 2: A Lexington Healthcare Company Mentors Local Startups

Resonate, Don't Just Connect:
Fostering Creative, Community-Driven Relationships in Louisville and Kentucky

In Lexington's growing healthcare sector, a well-established medical technology company has taken an active role in mentoring local healthcare startups. The company provides resources, advice, and networking opportunities to young entrepreneurs, helping them navigate the complexities of the healthcare industry.

While the larger company doesn't receive immediate financial returns from this mentorship, it has gained valuable insights into emerging trends and technologies by staying connected to the startup ecosystem. Additionally, several of the startups have gone on to become successful partners or collaborators, benefiting both the mentor company and the local healthcare community.

Case Study 3: A Louisville Manufacturer Collaborates on Workforce Development

In Louisville's manufacturing sector, a local company has partnered with community colleges and vocational schools to develop workforce training programs that prepare students for careers in advanced manufacturing. By offering internships, apprenticeships, and job placement assistance, the company helps students gain practical experience while also building a pipeline of skilled workers.

This investment in workforce development benefits both the students and the company. The students gain valuable

Resonate, Don't Just Connect:
Fostering Creative, Community-Driven Relationships in Louisville and Kentucky

skills and career opportunities, while the company ensures a steady supply of qualified workers to support its growth. By offering value through education and training, the manufacturer strengthens its ties to the community and positions itself as a leader in workforce development.

5. Asking for Favors: When and How to Do It

While the focus of this chapter is on offering value first, there will come a time when you need to ask for favors or seek support from your network. When done appropriately, asking for favors is a natural part of any business relationship, especially when you've already established trust and reciprocity.

Timing is Everything

The key to asking for favors is timing. It's important to build a strong foundation of giving before making a request. If you've consistently offered value, helped others, and built genuine relationships, your network will be more likely to support you when you need it.

For example, if you've spent years mentoring a colleague or supporting a business partner, they will be more inclined to help you when you need an introduction, advice, or support with a project.

Be Specific and Thoughtful

Resonate, Don't Just Connect:
Fostering Creative, Community-Driven Relationships in Louisville and Kentucky

When asking for a favor, be specific about what you need and why. Make it easy for the other person to understand how they can help, and be mindful of their time and resources.

For example, if you're asking for an introduction to a potential client in Kentucky's healthcare sector, you might say:

"Hi [Name],
I hope you're doing well. I've been working on expanding my healthcare consulting business, and I noticed that you have a connection with [Client Name] at [Company]. If you think it's appropriate, I'd greatly appreciate an introduction. Of course, if there's anything I can do to return the favor, please let me know!
Best regards,
[Your Name]"

By being specific and thoughtful, you make it easier for the other person to help you, while also showing that you value their time and effort.

Always Offer to Reciprocate

Even when asking for favors, it's important to continue offering value. When making a request, always offer to reciprocate in some way. This reinforces the idea that your relationship is built on mutual benefit, not just one-sided requests.

Resonate, Don't Just Connect:
Fostering Creative, Community-Driven Relationships in Louisville and Kentucky

For example:

"If there's anything I can do to help you with your upcoming project, please don't hesitate to reach out. I'd be happy to assist in any way I can."

This shows that you are still committed to the principle of giving, even when you're the one asking for help.

Conclusion: The Business of Giving in Kentucky

In Kentucky, where business is often built on relationships, trust, and community, the principle of offering value before asking for favors is essential for long-term success. By focusing on giving—whether through sharing knowledge, making connections, providing resources, or mentoring others—you create a network of trusted partners who are more than willing to support you when the time comes.

The business of giving is not just about immediate gains; it's about building a foundation for sustainable growth, mutual benefit, and lasting relationships. In Kentucky's diverse industries, from bourbon and agriculture to healthcare and manufacturing, this approach aligns with the state's core values of collaboration, community, and trust.

By embracing the philosophy of giving first, you not only enhance your own business success but also contribute to

Resonate, Don't Just Connect:
Fostering Creative, Community-Driven Relationships in Louisville and Kentucky

the success of those around you, creating a stronger, more resilient business community for all.

Resonate, Don't Just Connect:
Fostering Creative, Community-Driven Relationships in Louisville and Kentucky

Chapter 10: Measuring the ROI of Networking – Tracking the Real Business Outcomes of Your Connections

In Kentucky, where business is often built on trust, community ties, and long-term relationships, networking is more than just exchanging business cards or attending events; it's about cultivating meaningful connections that lead to tangible business outcomes. However, despite the widespread understanding of the importance of networking, many professionals struggle to measure its return on investment (ROI). How do you quantify the value of a handshake, a referral, or a relationship that may not pay off immediately but holds long-term potential?

The challenge of measuring the ROI of networking is that it often involves intangible benefits—like trust, goodwill, and reputation—that don't directly translate into immediate financial returns. But in Kentucky, where industries like bourbon, healthcare, agriculture, and logistics thrive on relationships, the impact of networking can be seen in the form of new partnerships, client acquisitions, career advancements, and community influence. The key to understanding the true value of your network lies in tracking these real business outcomes and identifying the long-term benefits that your connections provide.

Resonate, Don't Just Connect:
Fostering Creative, Community-Driven Relationships in Louisville and Kentucky

In this chapter, we will explore how to measure the ROI of networking in practical terms. We'll discuss specific metrics to track, strategies for maximizing the value of your connections, and how to align your networking efforts with your business goals. By the end, you'll have a clearer picture of how to quantify the success of your networking activities and ensure that they contribute to your growth, both personally and professionally.

1. The Importance of Measuring Networking ROI

While networking is often seen as a soft skill, it's essential to treat it like any other business investment. Just as you would measure the success of a marketing campaign or a financial investment, it's important to assess the impact of your networking efforts. Understanding the ROI of networking can help you determine whether your time and resources are being spent effectively and guide your strategy for building relationships that generate real business outcomes.

Why Networking ROI Matters

In Kentucky's interconnected business landscape, where relationships can open doors to new opportunities, measuring networking ROI is particularly important. The state's key industries—such as bourbon, healthcare, and logistics—rely heavily on personal connections, partnerships, and community involvement. Knowing how your network contributes to these outcomes allows you to

Resonate, Don't Just Connect:
Fostering Creative, Community-Driven Relationships in Louisville and Kentucky

make informed decisions about where to invest your time and effort.

There are several reasons why measuring networking ROI is essential:

- **Resource Allocation**: Networking takes time, effort, and sometimes money. By measuring its ROI, you can ensure that your resources are being used effectively and that you're focusing on the connections that provide the most value.

- **Strategic Focus**: Tracking networking outcomes helps you identify which relationships and activities are contributing to your business goals, allowing you to focus on building the right kinds of connections.

- **Long-Term Success**: Networking often leads to long-term opportunities that aren't immediately apparent. By measuring ROI, you can recognize the full value of your connections over time, even if they don't result in immediate financial gains.

In Kentucky's bourbon industry, for example, long-term relationships with suppliers, distributors, and retailers are essential for business growth. Measuring the ROI of these relationships can help you understand the value they bring in terms of sales, brand reputation, and market expansion.

2. Key Metrics for Measuring Networking ROI

Resonate, Don't Just Connect:
Fostering Creative, Community-Driven Relationships in Louisville and Kentucky

Measuring the ROI of networking requires looking at both quantitative and qualitative metrics. While some outcomes, like revenue or client acquisition, can be easily quantified, others, such as trust, reputation, and influence, are more difficult to measure but are equally important.

Here are some key metrics to consider when evaluating the ROI of your networking efforts:

1. Revenue Generation

One of the most direct ways to measure networking ROI is by tracking how your connections contribute to revenue generation. This can include new business deals, client referrals, or partnerships that result in increased sales. In Kentucky's business landscape, where relationships often lead to new business opportunities, this metric is particularly relevant.

For example, if you run a healthcare business in Lexington and a connection you made at a local industry conference leads to a new client contract, you can directly attribute that revenue to your networking efforts. Tracking these outcomes over time allows you to see how your relationships contribute to your bottom line.

To measure revenue generation from networking:

- **Track client sources**: When acquiring new clients, track how you were introduced to them. Was it through a networking event, a referral from

Resonate, Don't Just Connect:
Fostering Creative, Community-Driven Relationships in Louisville and Kentucky

a colleague, or a connection made through a business partner?

- **Monitor sales increases**: Look for patterns where your networking efforts have contributed to sales growth. This could be through direct client referrals or partnerships that expand your reach.

2. New Business Opportunities and Partnerships

Networking often leads to new business opportunities, whether it's through collaborations, partnerships, or access to new markets. In Kentucky's business environment, where partnerships between industries like bourbon, agriculture, and manufacturing are common, tracking these opportunities is a key measure of networking success.

For instance, if you're in the logistics industry and a connection you made at a Kentucky Chamber of Commerce event leads to a partnership with a local manufacturer, this represents a clear business outcome from your networking efforts. These types of partnerships can lead to increased efficiency, expanded services, and shared resources that benefit both parties.

To track new business opportunities:

- **Document collaborations**: Keep a record of any partnerships or joint ventures that resulted from

Resonate, Don't Just Connect:
Fostering Creative, Community-Driven Relationships in Louisville and Kentucky

your networking efforts. Note the financial and operational benefits of these collaborations.

- **Assess market expansion**: If networking has helped you enter new markets or expand your business footprint, track the impact of these efforts on your overall growth.

3. Referrals and Recommendations

Referrals are a powerful outcome of networking, particularly in Kentucky's close-knit business communities. When someone in your network refers a client, partner, or job opportunity to you, it's a direct result of the trust and goodwill you've built through your relationships.

In industries like healthcare or real estate, where trust is paramount, referrals can be one of the most valuable metrics of networking ROI. For example, if a doctor in Louisville refers patients to a specialist they met at a medical conference, this referral can lead to increased business for the specialist and strengthen the relationship between the two professionals.

To measure the impact of referrals:

- **Track referral sources**: When a new client or partner is referred to you, note who made the referral and how that connection was established.

Resonate, Don't Just Connect:
Fostering Creative, Community-Driven Relationships in Louisville and Kentucky

This helps you understand which relationships are contributing the most value.

- **Monitor referral frequency**: If you're receiving a high volume of referrals from a specific network or group, this indicates that your networking efforts are paying off in terms of trust and influence.

4. Influence and Reputation

While influence and reputation are more difficult to quantify, they are critical factors in measuring networking ROI. In Kentucky's business culture, where reputation often precedes you, building influence within your industry or community can lead to long-term benefits such as leadership opportunities, speaking engagements, or invitations to join boards or committees.

For example, if you're a thought leader in Kentucky's education sector and your influence leads to an invitation to speak at a major conference, this opportunity enhances your visibility and opens doors to new connections and collaborations. While this may not result in immediate revenue, it positions you as a key player in your industry, which can lead to future opportunities.

To assess your influence and reputation:

- **Track speaking engagements or leadership roles**: Document any invitations to speak at

Resonate, Don't Just Connect:
Fostering Creative, Community-Driven Relationships in Louisville and Kentucky

events, join advisory boards, or lead industry panels. These opportunities are indicators of your growing influence within your network.

- **Monitor media mentions or recognition**: If your networking efforts lead to media coverage, awards, or recognition within your industry, these are signs that your reputation is strengthening.

5. Career Advancement and Job Opportunities

For individuals, networking is often a key driver of career advancement. In Kentucky's business landscape, where many industries are interconnected, building a strong network can lead to new job opportunities, promotions, or mentorships that enhance your professional growth.

If a connection you made through a local business association helps you land a new job or secure a promotion, this is a clear example of networking ROI. Similarly, if a mentor you connected with through a networking event provides guidance that leads to career advancement, this mentorship represents a valuable outcome of your efforts.

To track career advancement:

- **Document new job opportunities**: If you secure a new job or promotion through your network, note how that opportunity was facilitated by your connections.

- **Assess mentorship benefits**: If a mentor or advisor has played a key role in your professional growth, track the specific ways in which their guidance has impacted your career.

6. Time and Cost Savings

Networking can also lead to operational efficiencies and cost savings, particularly when it comes to finding trusted suppliers, partners, or service providers. In Kentucky's manufacturing or logistics industries, for example, building relationships with suppliers who offer favorable terms or faster delivery times can have a direct impact on your bottom line.

If networking helps you find a more cost-effective solution to a business challenge—whether it's through a partnership, a referral, or access to industry knowledge—this represents a tangible return on your investment. Over time, these savings can accumulate and contribute to your overall business success.

To measure time and cost savings:

- **Track supplier or service provider relationships**: Document any cost savings or efficiency gains that result from networking relationships, such as finding a more affordable supplier or streamlining your operations through a partnership.

Resonate, Don't Just Connect:
Fostering Creative, Community-Driven Relationships in Louisville and Kentucky

- **Assess time savings**: If networking helps you solve a problem more quickly or access resources that save time, track these benefits as part of your overall ROI.

3. Strategies for Maximizing Networking ROI

Once you understand how to measure the ROI of networking, the next step is to implement strategies that maximize the value of your connections. In Kentucky, where business is often based on long-term relationships and community ties, the following strategies can help you build a network that contributes to your success.

1. Align Networking with Business Goals

To maximize the ROI of networking, it's essential to align your efforts with your business goals. This means being intentional about who you connect with, where you network, and what outcomes you're seeking from your relationships.

For example, if your goal is to expand your bourbon business into new markets, focus on networking with distributors, retailers, and industry leaders who can help facilitate that growth. By aligning your networking efforts with specific business objectives, you can ensure that your connections are contributing to measurable outcomes.

Resonate, Don't Just Connect:
Fostering Creative, Community-Driven Relationships in Louisville and Kentucky

In Kentucky's healthcare sector, aligning networking with business goals might involve building relationships with hospital administrators or insurance providers who can help you navigate the regulatory landscape and secure new contracts.

2. Be Consistent and Persistent

Networking is not a one-time activity—it requires consistency and persistence over time. Building strong relationships takes effort, and it's important to stay engaged with your network, even when you're not actively seeking opportunities.

In Kentucky, where personal relationships are often the foundation of business success, maintaining regular contact with your connections is essential. This can involve attending industry events, following up with emails or calls, and offering value to your network without expecting immediate returns.

For example, if you're in the agriculture industry, staying in touch with local farmers, suppliers, and industry leaders through regular meetings or community events helps keep your relationships strong and ensures that you're top of mind when opportunities arise.

3. Diversify Your Network

To maximize networking ROI, it's important to build a diverse network that spans multiple industries, regions,

Resonate, Don't Just Connect:
Fostering Creative, Community-Driven Relationships in Louisville and Kentucky

and professional levels. In Kentucky, where industries like healthcare, bourbon, agriculture, and logistics are closely connected, having a diverse network can open doors to unexpected opportunities.

For example, if you work in Kentucky's manufacturing sector, expanding your network to include logistics professionals, tech innovators, or even local government officials can help you access new resources and partnerships that support your business growth.

Diversifying your network also helps protect against economic downturns or industry-specific challenges. By building relationships across multiple sectors, you ensure that your network remains valuable even when certain industries face challenges.

4. Offer Value Before Asking for Favors

One of the most effective ways to build strong, reciprocal relationships is by offering value before asking for favors. In Kentucky's business culture, where trust and community are central, being generous with your time, knowledge, and resources can help you establish a reputation as someone who contributes to the success of others.

For example, if you're a real estate professional in Louisville, offering to share market insights, introduce clients, or collaborate on community projects helps you

Resonate, Don't Just Connect:
Fostering Creative, Community-Driven Relationships in Louisville and Kentucky

build goodwill within your network. When the time comes to ask for support, your network will be more willing to help because you've already demonstrated your value.

5. Follow Up and Nurture Relationships

Following up after networking events or introductions is crucial for turning initial connections into long-term relationships. In Kentucky, where relationships often develop over time, consistent follow-up is essential for nurturing connections and keeping your network engaged.

Whether it's sending a thank-you note after a meeting, following up on a conversation from a conference, or offering to meet for coffee, taking the time to nurture your relationships helps build trust and ensures that your network remains active.

For example, if you meet someone at a healthcare summit in Lexington, following up with an email that references your conversation and suggests future collaboration helps keep the relationship moving forward.

4. Case Studies: Networking ROI in Kentucky

To illustrate how networking ROI can be measured and maximized in Kentucky's unique business environment, let's look at a few case studies from key industries.

Resonate, Don't Just Connect:
Fostering Creative, Community-Driven Relationships in Louisville and Kentucky

Case Study 1: A Bourbon Distillery Expands into New Markets

A small bourbon distillery in Bardstown sought to expand its distribution into new states. By attending industry events and networking with distributors and retailers, the distillery's owner built relationships that eventually led to new distribution deals in several key markets.

The owner tracked the revenue generated from these new markets and identified that the connections made at industry events directly contributed to a 20% increase in sales over the next two years. By aligning networking efforts with the goal of market expansion, the distillery achieved measurable success.

Case Study 2: A Healthcare Professional Gains Career Advancement

A healthcare executive in Louisville attended a leadership conference where she connected with industry leaders and mentors. Through these relationships, she gained valuable career guidance and eventually received a recommendation for a leadership role at a major hospital.

By tracking her career advancement and the role that her network played in securing the job, the executive was able to measure the impact of her networking efforts on her professional growth. The mentorship and referrals she received through her network contributed directly to her promotion.

Case Study 3: A Logistics Company Reduces Costs Through Supplier Relationships

A logistics company in Northern Kentucky built strong relationships with local suppliers by attending industry events and joining regional business associations. Through these connections, the company was able to negotiate better pricing and improve delivery times, resulting in significant cost savings.

By tracking the financial impact of these partnerships, the company identified that networking had reduced its supply chain costs by 15%, contributing to overall business efficiency and profitability.

5. The Long-Term Value of Networking

While many of the benefits of networking can be measured in immediate outcomes like revenue generation or client acquisition, it's important to recognize the long-term value of building strong relationships. Networking ROI often compounds over time as relationships deepen, trust builds, and new opportunities arise.

In Kentucky's business culture, where community and relationships are central to success, networking is a long-term investment that pays dividends in both tangible and intangible ways. By consistently offering value, nurturing

Resonate, Don't Just Connect:
Fostering Creative, Community-Driven Relationships in Louisville and Kentucky

your relationships, and tracking the outcomes of your networking efforts, you can ensure that your network contributes to your growth and success for years to come.

Conclusion: Tracking the ROI of Networking in Kentucky

Measuring the ROI of networking is crucial for understanding the true value of your connections and ensuring that your efforts contribute to your business goals. In Kentucky, where relationships and community ties are essential to business success, tracking both the tangible and intangible outcomes of your networking activities helps you make informed decisions about where to invest your time and resources.

By focusing on key metrics like revenue generation, new business opportunities, referrals, and career advancement, you can quantify the impact of your network on your success. Additionally, implementing strategies that maximize networking ROI—such as aligning networking with business goals, offering value, and nurturing relationships—ensures that your network continues to provide long-term benefits.

Ultimately, networking in Kentucky is about more than just making connections—it's about building lasting relationships that contribute to the success of everyone involved. By measuring and maximizing the ROI of your networking efforts, you can create a network that supports

Resonate, Don't Just Connect:
Fostering Creative, Community-Driven Relationships in Louisville and Kentucky

your growth, enhances your reputation, and drives business outcomes for years to come.

Resonate, Don't Just Connect:
Fostering Creative, Community-Driven Relationships in Louisville and Kentucky

Chapter 10: Measuring the ROI of Networking – Tracking the Real Business Outcomes of Your Connections

In Kentucky, where business is often built on trust, community ties, and long-term relationships, networking is more than just exchanging business cards or attending events; it's about cultivating meaningful connections that lead to tangible business outcomes. However, despite the widespread understanding of the importance of networking, many professionals struggle to measure its return on investment (ROI). How do you quantify the value of a handshake, a referral, or a relationship that may not pay off immediately but holds long-term potential?

The challenge of measuring the ROI of networking is that it often involves intangible benefits—like trust, goodwill, and reputation—that don't directly translate into immediate financial returns. But in Kentucky, where industries like bourbon, healthcare, agriculture, and logistics thrive on relationships, the impact of networking can be seen in the form of new partnerships, client acquisitions, career advancements, and community influence. The key to understanding the true value of your network lies in tracking these real business outcomes and

Resonate, Don't Just Connect:
Fostering Creative, Community-Driven Relationships in Louisville and Kentucky

identifying the long-term benefits that your connections provide.

In this chapter, we will explore how to measure the ROI of networking in practical terms. We'll discuss specific metrics to track, strategies for maximizing the value of your connections, and how to align your networking efforts with your business goals. By the end, you'll have a clearer picture of how to quantify the success of your networking activities and ensure that they contribute to your growth, both personally and professionally.

1. The Importance of Measuring Networking ROI

While networking is often seen as a soft skill, it's essential to treat it like any other business investment. Just as you would measure the success of a marketing campaign or a financial investment, it's important to assess the impact of your networking efforts. Understanding the ROI of networking can help you determine whether your time and resources are being spent effectively and guide your strategy for building relationships that generate real business outcomes.

Why Networking ROI Matters

In Kentucky's interconnected business landscape, where relationships can open doors to new opportunities, measuring networking ROI is particularly important. The state's key industries—such as bourbon, healthcare, and

Resonate, Don't Just Connect:
Fostering Creative, Community-Driven Relationships in Louisville and Kentucky

logistics—rely heavily on personal connections, partnerships, and community involvement. Knowing how your network contributes to these outcomes allows you to make informed decisions about where to invest your time and effort.

There are several reasons why measuring networking ROI is essential:

- **Resource Allocation**: Networking takes time, effort, and sometimes money. By measuring its ROI, you can ensure that your resources are being used effectively and that you're focusing on the connections that provide the most value.

- **Strategic Focus**: Tracking networking outcomes helps you identify which relationships and activities are contributing to your business goals, allowing you to focus on building the right kinds of connections.

- **Long-Term Success**: Networking often leads to long-term opportunities that aren't immediately apparent. By measuring ROI, you can recognize the full value of your connections over time, even if they don't result in immediate financial gains.

In Kentucky's bourbon industry, for example, long-term relationships with suppliers, distributors, and retailers are essential for business growth. Measuring the ROI of these

Resonate, Don't Just Connect:
Fostering Creative, Community-Driven Relationships in Louisville and Kentucky

relationships can help you understand the value they bring in terms of sales, brand reputation, and market expansion.

2. Key Metrics for Measuring Networking ROI

Measuring the ROI of networking requires looking at both quantitative and qualitative metrics. While some outcomes, like revenue or client acquisition, can be easily quantified, others, such as trust, reputation, and influence, are more difficult to measure but are equally important.

Here are some key metrics to consider when evaluating the ROI of your networking efforts:

1. Revenue Generation

One of the most direct ways to measure networking ROI is by tracking how your connections contribute to revenue generation. This can include new business deals, client referrals, or partnerships that result in increased sales. In Kentucky's business landscape, where relationships often lead to new business opportunities, this metric is particularly relevant.

For example, if you run a healthcare business in Lexington and a connection you made at a local industry conference leads to a new client contract, you can directly attribute that revenue to your networking efforts. Tracking these outcomes over time allows you to see how your relationships contribute to your bottom line.

Resonate, Don't Just Connect:
Fostering Creative, Community-Driven Relationships in Louisville and Kentucky

To measure revenue generation from networking:

- **Track client sources**: When acquiring new clients, track how you were introduced to them. Was it through a networking event, a referral from a colleague, or a connection made through a business partner?

- **Monitor sales increases**: Look for patterns where your networking efforts have contributed to sales growth. This could be through direct client referrals or partnerships that expand your reach.

2. New Business Opportunities and Partnerships

Networking often leads to new business opportunities, whether it's through collaborations, partnerships, or access to new markets. In Kentucky's business environment, where partnerships between industries like bourbon, agriculture, and manufacturing are common, tracking these opportunities is a key measure of networking success.

For instance, if you're in the logistics industry and a connection you made at a Kentucky Chamber of Commerce event leads to a partnership with a local manufacturer, this represents a clear business outcome from your networking efforts. These types of partnerships can lead to increased efficiency, expanded services, and shared resources that benefit both parties.

Resonate, Don't Just Connect:
Fostering Creative, Community-Driven Relationships in Louisville and Kentucky

To track new business opportunities:

- **Document collaborations**: Keep a record of any partnerships or joint ventures that resulted from your networking efforts. Note the financial and operational benefits of these collaborations.

- **Assess market expansion**: If networking has helped you enter new markets or expand your business footprint, track the impact of these efforts on your overall growth.

3. Referrals and Recommendations

Referrals are a powerful outcome of networking, particularly in Kentucky's close-knit business communities. When someone in your network refers a client, partner, or job opportunity to you, it's a direct result of the trust and goodwill you've built through your relationships.

In industries like healthcare or real estate, where trust is paramount, referrals can be one of the most valuable metrics of networking ROI. For example, if a doctor in Louisville refers patients to a specialist they met at a medical conference, this referral can lead to increased business for the specialist and strengthen the relationship between the two professionals.

To measure the impact of referrals:

Resonate, Don't Just Connect:
Fostering Creative, Community-Driven Relationships in Louisville and Kentucky

- **Track referral sources**: When a new client or partner is referred to you, note who made the referral and how that connection was established. This helps you understand which relationships are contributing the most value.

- **Monitor referral frequency**: If you're receiving a high volume of referrals from a specific network or group, this indicates that your networking efforts are paying off in terms of trust and influence.

4. Influence and Reputation

While influence and reputation are more difficult to quantify, they are critical factors in measuring networking ROI. In Kentucky's business culture, where reputation often precedes you, building influence within your industry or community can lead to long-term benefits such as leadership opportunities, speaking engagements, or invitations to join boards or committees.

For example, if you're a thought leader in Kentucky's education sector and your influence leads to an invitation to speak at a major conference, this opportunity enhances your visibility and opens doors to new connections and collaborations. While this may not result in immediate revenue, it positions you as a key player in your industry, which can lead to future opportunities.

Resonate, Don't Just Connect:
Fostering Creative, Community-Driven Relationships in Louisville and Kentucky

To assess your influence and reputation:

- **Track speaking engagements or leadership roles**: Document any invitations to speak at events, join advisory boards, or lead industry panels. These opportunities are indicators of your growing influence within your network.

- **Monitor media mentions or recognition**: If your networking efforts lead to media coverage, awards, or recognition within your industry, these are signs that your reputation is strengthening.

5. Career Advancement and Job Opportunities

For individuals, networking is often a key driver of career advancement. In Kentucky's business landscape, where many industries are interconnected, building a strong network can lead to new job opportunities, promotions, or mentorships that enhance your professional growth.

If a connection you made through a local business association helps you land a new job or secure a promotion, this is a clear example of networking ROI. Similarly, if a mentor you connected with through a networking event provides guidance that leads to career advancement, this mentorship represents a valuable outcome of your efforts.

To track career advancement:

Resonate, Don't Just Connect:
Fostering Creative, Community-Driven Relationships in Louisville and Kentucky

- **Document new job opportunities**: If you secure a new job or promotion through your network, note how that opportunity was facilitated by your connections.

- **Assess mentorship benefits**: If a mentor or advisor has played a key role in your professional growth, track the specific ways in which their guidance has impacted your career.

6. Time and Cost Savings

Networking can also lead to operational efficiencies and cost savings, particularly when it comes to finding trusted suppliers, partners, or service providers. In Kentucky's manufacturing or logistics industries, for example, building relationships with suppliers who offer favorable terms or faster delivery times can have a direct impact on your bottom line.

If networking helps you find a more cost-effective solution to a business challenge—whether it's through a partnership, a referral, or access to industry knowledge—this represents a tangible return on your investment. Over time, these savings can accumulate and contribute to your overall business success.

To measure time and cost savings:

- **Track supplier or service provider relationships**: Document any cost savings or efficiency gains that result from networking relationships, such as finding a more affordable supplier or streamlining your operations through a partnership.

- **Assess time savings**: If networking helps you solve a problem more quickly or access resources that save time, track these benefits as part of your overall ROI.

3. Strategies for Maximizing Networking ROI

Once you understand how to measure the ROI of networking, the next step is to implement strategies that maximize the value of your connections. In Kentucky, where business is often based on long-term relationships and community ties, the following strategies can help you build a network that contributes to your success.

1. Align Networking with Business Goals

To maximize the ROI of networking, it's essential to align your efforts with your business goals. This means being intentional about who you connect with, where you network, and what outcomes you're seeking from your relationships.

For example, if your goal is to expand your bourbon business into new markets, focus on networking with distributors, retailers, and industry leaders who can help facilitate that growth. By aligning your networking efforts

Resonate, Don't Just Connect:
Fostering Creative, Community-Driven Relationships in Louisville and Kentucky

with specific business objectives, you can ensure that your connections are contributing to measurable outcomes.

In Kentucky's healthcare sector, aligning networking with business goals might involve building relationships with hospital administrators or insurance providers who can help you navigate the regulatory landscape and secure new contracts.

2. Be Consistent and Persistent

Networking is not a one-time activity—it requires consistency and persistence over time. Building strong relationships takes effort, and it's important to stay engaged with your network, even when you're not actively seeking opportunities.

In Kentucky, where personal relationships are often the foundation of business success, maintaining regular contact with your connections is essential. This can involve attending industry events, following up with emails or calls, and offering value to your network without expecting immediate returns.

For example, if you're in the agriculture industry, staying in touch with local farmers, suppliers, and industry leaders through regular meetings or community events helps keep your relationships strong and ensures that you're top of mind when opportunities arise.

Resonate, Don't Just Connect:
Fostering Creative, Community-Driven Relationships in Louisville and Kentucky

3. Diversify Your Network

To maximize networking ROI, it's important to build a diverse network that spans multiple industries, regions, and professional levels. In Kentucky, where industries like healthcare, bourbon, agriculture, and logistics are closely connected, having a diverse network can open doors to unexpected opportunities.

For example, if you work in Kentucky's manufacturing sector, expanding your network to include logistics professionals, tech innovators, or even local government officials can help you access new resources and partnerships that support your business growth.

Diversifying your network also helps protect against economic downturns or industry-specific challenges. By building relationships across multiple sectors, you ensure that your network remains valuable even when certain industries face challenges.

4. Offer Value Before Asking for Favors

One of the most effective ways to build strong, reciprocal relationships is by offering value before asking for favors. In Kentucky's business culture, where trust and community are central, being generous with your time, knowledge, and resources can help you establish a reputation as someone who contributes to the success of others.

Resonate, Don't Just Connect:
Fostering Creative, Community-Driven Relationships in Louisville and Kentucky

For example, if you're a real estate professional in Louisville, offering to share market insights, introduce clients, or collaborate on community projects helps you build goodwill within your network. When the time comes to ask for support, your network will be more willing to help because you've already demonstrated your value.

5. Follow Up and Nurture Relationships

Following up after networking events or introductions is crucial for turning initial connections into long-term relationships. In Kentucky, where relationships often develop over time, consistent follow-up is essential for nurturing connections and keeping your network engaged.

Whether it's sending a thank-you note after a meeting, following up on a conversation from a conference, or offering to meet for coffee, taking the time to nurture your relationships helps build trust and ensures that your network remains active.

For example, if you meet someone at a healthcare summit in Lexington, following up with an email that references your conversation and suggests future collaboration helps keep the relationship moving forward.

4. Case Studies: Networking ROI in Kentucky

Resonate, Don't Just Connect:
Fostering Creative, Community-Driven Relationships in Louisville and Kentucky

To illustrate how networking ROI can be measured and maximized in Kentucky's unique business environment, let's look at a few case studies from key industries.

Case Study 1: A Bourbon Distillery Expands into New Markets

A small bourbon distillery in Bardstown sought to expand its distribution into new states. By attending industry events and networking with distributors and retailers, the distillery's owner built relationships that eventually led to new distribution deals in several key markets.

The owner tracked the revenue generated from these new markets and identified that the connections made at industry events directly contributed to a 20% increase in sales over the next two years. By aligning networking efforts with the goal of market expansion, the distillery achieved measurable success.

Case Study 2: A Healthcare Professional Gains Career Advancement

A healthcare executive in Louisville attended a leadership conference where she connected with industry leaders and mentors. Through these relationships, she gained valuable career guidance and eventually received a recommendation for a leadership role at a major hospital.

By tracking her career advancement and the role that her network played in securing the job, the executive was able

Resonate, Don't Just Connect:
Fostering Creative, Community-Driven Relationships in Louisville and Kentucky

to measure the impact of her networking efforts on her professional growth. The mentorship and referrals she received through her network contributed directly to her promotion.

Case Study 3: A Logistics Company Reduces Costs Through Supplier Relationships

A logistics company in Northern Kentucky built strong relationships with local suppliers by attending industry events and joining regional business associations. Through these connections, the company was able to negotiate better pricing and improve delivery times, resulting in significant cost savings.

By tracking the financial impact of these partnerships, the company identified that networking had reduced its supply chain costs by 15%, contributing to overall business efficiency and profitability.

5. The Long-Term Value of Networking

While many of the benefits of networking can be measured in immediate outcomes like revenue generation or client acquisition, it's important to recognize the long-term value of building strong relationships. Networking ROI often compounds over time as relationships deepen, trust builds, and new opportunities arise.

In Kentucky's business culture, where community and relationships are central to success, networking is a long-

Resonate, Don't Just Connect:
Fostering Creative, Community-Driven Relationships in Louisville and Kentucky

term investment that pays dividends in both tangible and intangible ways. By consistently offering value, nurturing your relationships, and tracking the outcomes of your networking efforts, you can ensure that your network contributes to your growth and success for years to come.

Conclusion: Tracking the ROI of Networking in Kentucky

Measuring the ROI of networking is crucial for understanding the true value of your connections and ensuring that your efforts contribute to your business goals. In Kentucky, where relationships and community ties are essential to business success, tracking both the tangible and intangible outcomes of your networking activities helps you make informed decisions about where to invest your time and resources.

By focusing on key metrics like revenue generation, new business opportunities, referrals, and career advancement, you can quantify the impact of your network on your success. Additionally, implementing strategies that maximize networking ROI—such as aligning networking with business goals, offering value, and nurturing relationships—ensures that your network continues to provide long-term benefits.

Ultimately, networking in Kentucky is about more than just making connections—it's about building lasting relationships that contribute to the success of everyone

Resonate, Don't Just Connect:
Fostering Creative, Community-Driven Relationships in Louisville and Kentucky

involved. By measuring and maximizing the ROI of your networking efforts, you can create a network that supports your growth, enhances your reputation, and drives business outcomes for years to come.

Resonate, Don't Just Connect:
Fostering Creative, Community-Driven Relationships in Louisville and Kentucky

The End

Thank You

"Don't just connect—resonate with each person on a human level; that's when creativity and talent between you come together to truly add value to the community." –
Di Tran

www.ingramcontent.com/pod-product-compliance
Lightning Source LLC
Chambersburg PA
CBHW052202220526
45471CB00004B/1775